Ruth Scott is a freelance writer, broadcaster, lecturer and facilitator whose disparate areas of work are united by the theme of storytelling. She was among the first women to be ordained priest in the Church of England in 1994, and is now a member of the Quakers. She has written drama and reflective programmes for the BBC World Service and Radio 4, and broadcasts regularly on Radio 2's 'Pause for Thought' and *Good Morning Sunday*.

Still

THE POWER OF IMPERFECTION

Ruth Scott

First published in Great Britain in 2014

Society for Promoting Christian Knowledge
36 Causton Street
London SW1P 4ST
www.spckpublishing.co.uk

The author and publisher have made every effort to ensure that the external website and
email addresses included in this book are correct and up to date at the time of going
to press. The author and publisher are not responsible for the content, quality or
continuing accessibility of the sites.

British Library Cataloguing-in-Publication Data
A catalogue record for this book is available from the British Library

ISBN 978–0–281–07307–8
eBook ISBN 978–0–281–07308–5

Typeset by Graphicraft Limited, Hong Kong
First printed in Great Britain by Ashford Colour Press
Subsequently digitally printed in Great Britain

eBook by Graphicraft Limited, Hong Kong

Produced on paper from sustainable forests

Contents

Contents

Acknowledgements

This book would not have been possible without Chris and Alison. Chris, my deep, still water, thank you for sharing the journey and loving me no matter what. Alison, my sanctuary through Narnian winter, thank you for your constant friendship. I owe you my sanity, such as it is.

Thank you Freya and Tian. You have unconsciously taught me so much.

Thank you, Rowan, for being the 'reader-over-my-shoulder' in the early stages, despite an already jam-packed diary. Your gentle and perceptive feedback sparked trains of thought that made this book better than it might otherwise have been.

Thank you, Rachel and Melanie, for reading the first draft and sharing your reflections about it with me with care and sensitive honesty.

Thank you to the team at SPCK, particularly Alison Barr. Your calm and constructive responses enabled easy passage through the process of publication.

Finally, thank you to all those people over the years who have helped me to live and work with who I am in all my messiness and complexity. The names of some are inscribed on my heart. The names of others are unknown because we met in passing and you have no idea about the impact you had upon me.

Introduction

I'm sitting in a BBC Radio 2 studio waiting to do my regular slot on the Chris Evans Breakfast Show. Chris's guest this morning is the wonderful English tenor Alfie Boe. On one side of Alfie sits BBC Sports reporter Vassos Alexander, a fixture on the show. I'm on the other side. Unlike everyone else in the studio, Vassos hasn't been reduced to tears by the tracks they've played of Alfie's songs, so Chris has asked Alfie to sing live in the studio, especially to Vassos. I'm on immediately afterwards with my 'Pause for Thought'.

At such close range, Alfie's singing vibrates through my body and leaves me choked up and breathless. How can I follow that? Yet follow it I must. As it happens I'm talking about the news item reporting that blue plaques marking the homes of famous people in London are about to become a thing of the past as a result of financial cutbacks. I wonder aloud what the plaques might have said if they had focused not on the amazing achievements of the person honoured, but on their way of *being*, and I suggest that might not be quite so edifying. Judging by the audible sounds coming from Chris and Alfie they agree. When I go on to ask what the three of us might find on such a plaque about ourselves, Chris laughs and says, 'Don't even go there!'

My script then continues as follows:

'Goodness' would definitely not be in a description of me. The best I might hope to be is a half-decent human being. 'Selfless' wouldn't figure either. Nor 'She hurt no one'. 'Could do better' is definitely on the cards, although it's a bit too negative for my liking. 'She tried to make something positive of her many mistakes' is much more realistic. Of course that's far too wordy for a small blue plaque. It's the kind of thing more likely to appear on my tombstone. Thinking about what we'd like to be remembered for, and what present reality suggests will be our legacy, can be a useful way of reflecting on where we're at and what changes in our behaviour we may need to think about. For this reason I'm glad my words might be for my epitaph. At least, hopefully, I shall have a few years yet to turn my mistakes into something more inspiringly memorable.

On the train home it suddenly strikes me that I could have produced a so much better script. I should have focused not on getting *beyond* my mistakes but on the creative potential of human complexity and messiness *as it is*. It's taken me long enough to realize the connection between my creativity and my complexity.

I am not where I expected to be in my mid-fifties. My younger self imagined me at my present age to be living a comfortable existence, free of material concerns and having sussed the meaning of life. My spirit of adventure would still be strong but wisdom and integrity of being would have calmed the restlessness of my youth. Given my reality today, the very thought of my earlier expectations makes me sit giggling at the computer; hysteria at the absurdity of it all finally setting in, no doubt! The memory is still strong of a recent anxiety dream in which I was standing in front of a congregation with hardly any clothes on, trying to read a service book that was disintegrating in my hands. The choir were revolting in the vestry. My sermon notes had disappeared, and there was a 50-foot rope to climb to get into the pulpit. Me, the epitome of calm and self-control? Not always! While those who listen to me on the radio, or who encounter me professionally and pastorally, perceive me as creative, gifted, calm, wise, strong, courageous and steadying, I and my close family and friends also know I can be erratic, emotional, unconfident, insecure, vulnerable, unreasonable and sometimes hard work. It's not that the person others perceive me to be is a pretence. It's simply that she's not the whole picture.

As if internal insecurity was not enough to deal with, recently I gave up my work as a chaplain in order to become fully freelance. I relinquished financial security to make room for . . . who knows what exactly! My head said this made no sense, but my heart felt it was the right thing to do. After 20 years of being a priest, ordained to priesthood with the first women in the Church of England, my spiritual home all my life, experience seems to be drawing me into the Society of Friends – the Quakers. The deepest love I know compels me along this path, but in moments of doubt I wonder if I've lost the plot completely.

In all these things there's a gap between my public face and my private experience. I wish that wasn't the case. I wish when I was confronted by my 17-year-old son pushing all my buttons, I was able always to activate my adult self, instead of sometimes behaving like an equally immature teenager. I wish the calm I bring to other people's problems was accessible always to me when confronting my own personal pain, instead of sometimes being commandeered by an inner crazy woman running amok through my life. I wish I could always think clearly and rationally, and not sometimes be overwhelmed by unhelpful and irrational emotions. At least, I wish these things when I'm confronted by their debilitating impact, but, again, it's not the whole picture.

It may not seem wise in the introduction to a book I want others to take seriously to highlight the inadequate aspects of who I am, but I want to counter right from the start the idea that a wise, generous and compassionate humanity depends upon a person being 'good', that is, free of the faults and failings wrestled with by the rest of us 'lesser' mortals. A number of times in my life people have said to me, 'Ruth, you're such a good person. I couldn't do what you do.' They couldn't be more wrong. While I'd love to be a better person than I am because messiness of being is, well, messy, and therefore painful not only for me but for those with whom my life connects deeply, the truth is the qualities I have that others value are the result of me working with, rather than by-passing, the broken aspects of my life. I know this also to be true of the men and women who have offered me the wisest counsel during the darkest times in my life.

The desire to put people on a pedestal, to see them as wholly good rather than deeply human, to value their light while denying its source in how they work with their darkness, is understandable, but it's also damaging. I was talking with a wonderful, accomplished woman in her seventies. A successful professional, she is the kind of person others seek out when they're looking for wise counsel. She's regarded highly in the community. Yet as we talked she spoke of how her younger self could not have imagined being in the position she now inhabits. She feels insecure, afraid and that, given some of the tough personal experiences she's had to endure, she's failed in some way. 'I can't say anything to other people,' she told me. 'Their lives are so together.' 'Or maybe,' I responded, 'they're feeling just as rattled as you are and, like you, are putting on a brave face and saying nothing of what they're really experiencing for fear of looking foolish or, worse still, becoming censured in some way by others who clearly have a better grip on things. Maybe they look at you and think how together your life seems to be compared to theirs, so they don't say anything either.'

My friend fears the more complex reality of who she is behind the face she presents to the world might provoke rejection from those she cares about, should she reveal it to them. It's an understandable concern. Many of us will know the experience of trusting another beloved human being with the person we are, warts and all, and of being rejected as a result of that. It's deeply scarring, and not the kind of experience we want to repeat. If that's the case with people we love, is it any wonder we are cautious about revealing vulnerability more widely?

Today's society is not a safe place to speak about our confusions and uncertainties, our complex natures and broken lives, at least not in any constructive way. There's any number of TV shows on which people can bear their souls in sensationalized storytelling, with the presenter manipulating the conversation in a prearranged direction and the audience booing the perceived bad guy as if they were at a Christmas pantomime. These tragic human farces are not seeking understanding. They're voyeuristic and cruel. Trial by audience is not the way to address human difficulties and dilemmas. For a so-called liberal society we are profoundly judgemental of human failing, as though we ourselves are squeaky clean, or maybe it's precisely because we can't accept we're not, that we come down heavily on similar inadequacies in others.

In 2012 the Leveson Inquiry reported its findings on the *News of the World* phone-hacking scandal, corruption relating to MPs' expenses rumbled on, the economic fallout of the banking world's greed and irresponsibility brought catastrophe to the lives of millions unable to make ends meet, lack of compassion and care in the NHS hit the head-lines, sex scandals in the Church or connected to the BBC shocked public sensibilities, and civil war in Syria escalated in ways that seemed increasingly impregnable to the possibility of peace-building. A few years down the line, these same stories persist or their themes continue to be played out in other contexts. Such examples of human failure and criminality rightly receive scrutiny and censure, but these stories are simply more extreme manifestations of the capacity for the abuse of power, invasion of privacy, greed, sexual confusion, conflict, cruelty and lack of compassion of which any one of us is capable. That we may lack the power to cause such a vast field of fallout does not deny our own ability to damage individual lives.

Baying for the blood of others who have screwed up big-time is infinitely easier than addressing our own messiness. Yet, how can we recognize and own our personal shades of grey in a society that often reacts as though human experience and ethics are black and white? Some of us, like my 70-year-old friend, are left feeling isolated and alone because we believe we're the only one whose life is messy and com-plicated. Some of us, unable to recognize complexity in ourselves, take up self-righteous positions of judgement against others who fall short. Fear of failure or the condemnation of others when we get things wrong may limit our lives to always playing it safe, but living a sanitized life is not the same as living a sanctified life.

In our society today, increasing numbers of people associate the inhumane rigidity of black and white thinking with what they perceive to be ignorant and outdated religion. In reality, the inability to understand complexity, contradiction and conflict is a human trait common to theists and atheists alike.

Like any other human institution, religion is not monochrome. While there may be aspects of it that quite rightly deserve challenge, criticism and rejection for being emotionally and intellectually unintelligent, religion has also inspired some of our greatest acts of compassion. It has played a central and positive part in my own life, not least because it continues to shed light for me on what it means to be human, at my worst and at my best.

I'm reminded of a friend, a Vietnam veteran who, while rejecting organized religion, found comfort and restoration in the Psalms, precisely because they articulated his deepest despair and pain and enabled him in some irrational but real way to feel 'held'. I know something of that experience too, and for this reason I have used relevant biblical stories in this book. The way I interpret them may not be how the original writer/s intended them to be understood, or how many people may interpret them today. Over the years I have understood a particular story in many different ways as my experience has changed and grown. The meaning of archetypal stories is not set in stone but emerges when we allow who we are to interact with the tale told. A conversation is opened up rather than closed down.

I know my 70-year-old friend and I are not alone in wrestling with the discrepancy between the people we'd like to be and the ones we actually are. In the course of my work I meet many men and women who struggle with imperfections of being they feel they can't talk about. Aware of my own confusions and shortcomings, I can at least provide a safe and caring space in which others may 'come clean'.

Compassion is crucial if we are to work creatively with our messiness of being. I say 'we' because in writing this book I'm making the assumption that whatever the differences between us of gender, race, creed, age and stage, sexual orientation, psychological type and mental health we share a common humanity. If this is the case then the chances are that you, like me, will have found being human is generally more complicated than you may have been raised to think or is generally acknowledged helpfully in the public domain.

I'll be asking more questions than I answer. Such answers as I have may not necessarily be right for you, whereas my questions may prompt more meaningful reflections of your own. My book aims simply to liberate those who read it from the feeling that everyone except themselves has life under control. I want to name some of the struggles many of us have with being human. By 'us' I mean people like me who want to live right but get things wrong despite our best intentions. I have hesitantly used personal stories as illustrations, not because they are extraordinary or edifying – far from it! It's what I know first-hand and since this book is about the private reality behind the public face we present to the world I think I should be prepared to speak a little about my own messiness. I'll explore the abuse of power, greed, sexual confusion, conflict, cruelty and lack of compassion of which any one of us is capable, and how we work with these things if we believe that perfection is neither possible nor preferable to the less than 'perfect' people we are. I shall argue that if we accepted a more realistic understanding of who we are, we would discover immense creativity in that acceptance.

Part 1

LEAVING EDEN

1

Paradise lost

———•◦•◦•———

I am a late developer. Adolescence passed me by. I moved from caring child to adult carer without encountering teenage rebellion. That came later when living through it was more complicated. As an adult I am supposed to know better, although I'm not sure I always do. Sometimes I think I simply find ways of concealing my confusion and appearing more together than I actually am. Sometimes I think I've got things sussed at last, only to fall flat on my face and feel back to square one! Ring any bells?

I didn't know myself truly as the woman I am until my late twenties when I moved to rural Herefordshire. My next-door neighbour was a wonderful and whacky woman, a one-time prima ballerina who by all accounts, in contrast to my own experience, had lived riotously and irreverently in the USA before retiring to renovate the dilapidated pile next door that was the rambling old rectory. Under her influence my long-term, short-cropped, 'worn out loo brush' look grew out, Rapunzel-style, to become a mane of strawberry blond hair long enough to sit on. In that transformation I came home to myself. The feminist part of me was unimpressed, but that's how it was. Human beings do not by nature fit into neat boxes or keep to the plot lines we think acceptable. As I indicated in my introduction, my own story has certainly not gone as I imagined it would in my youth.

Recognizing what is

My teenage self, with her romantic aspirations to sainthood, is a lifetime away. Back then I wanted to lead a selfless life. Inspired by my love for God I intended to do great things. I thought myself 'good', which must have been insufferable for my friends! I hadn't had to confront (or maybe I avoided) the less palatable aspects of my personality, so it was easy to condemn such things in others.

My stained-glass image of saints, like my sense of self, was far removed from reality. So many saints seem to have been neurotic, even mad, sometimes anarchic and usually difficult people. The fourteenth-century

St Catherine of Siena, for example, was anorexic. In her day her lack of appetite was considered miraculous. Today most of us would see it in far more down-to-earth terms. In that, I guess there's hope for us all. Sanctity is not about being free of human messiness. It's about drawing something magnificent out of the muddle. And yet we find the interconnectedness between the sordidness and sanctity of a person difficult to swallow.

That impulse to separate the darkness and light of our human nature is understandable. The darker disordered aspects of who we are, individually or collectively, can be profoundly destructive as well as potentially creative. Evidence of suffering imposed by one person on another, or one community on another, is all too apparent in human history. If you think about your own experiences of being hurt by, or hurting, others you will understand the impulse to deny or put at a distance the less palatable elements of being human. What possible good can come from them?

In 2014 I wrote a BBC Radio 4 Sunday Special for Holocaust Memorial Day. We recorded part of it in Auschwitz concentration camp in Poland, which confronts visitors with extreme acts of inhumanity. In the programme I was making, I wanted to help listeners recognize that the dynamics of dehumanizing and demonizing others in order to destroy them are not the sole preserve of evil, mad people but something of which we're all capable, albeit in less extreme forms for the most part. Back in England I interviewed four lovely Year 9 students from a school group visiting the Holocaust Centre at Laxton in Nottinghamshire.

'When students fall out with each other at school what happens?' I asked. They talked easily about how their language concerning the people they'd fallen out with became derogatory; how social media sites were used to abuse and alienate anyone who was seen as unacceptably different; how easy it was to join the bandwagon of people ganging up against a particular person; and how it was hard to speak out if you disagreed with what was happening because you might become the subject of bullying if you did.

Accepting who we are

I love the way the students were upfront about acknowledging behaviours in them and their friends that as adults we find harder to admit. The inability to own the way we can and do hurt others is far more destructive than if we're prepared to accept and work with the less palatable elements of who we are. Yet a common 'grown-up' response to this kind of honesty is to silence the one speaking with words of disapproval rather than recognize the truth of what they're saying and help them to make positive choices when confronted with human complexity.

Recently I was working with another group of 14-year-olds.

'What do you think or feel when you've hurt someone else?' I asked.

'Guilt,' 'Regret,' 'Sorry,' 'Angry,' and 'Anxious,' came up rapidly. Then there was a pause.

'Have any of you ever felt really glad when you've hurt another person?'

There were one or two nervous giggles as they glanced around at one another. No one spoke.

'Put up your hand', I said, 'if, like me, you've sometimes been glad your words or actions have hurt someone else because you think they deserved it.'

As soon as I raised my hand, there were sighs all round and a forest of hands went up.

'I thought so. These reactions are very human. It's not wrong that we have them. Generally we don't choose to feel them. The critical thing is what we do with them. We can follow through on them, adding to the harm of a situation, or we can decide to channel them in more constructive ways.'

To recognize the creative potential of working with our many shades of being is not to glorify grim realities or to say that anything goes. It's about equipping us to work with what is rather than denying it or beating ourselves up because we're not the person we'd like to be.

As a child growing up in a practising Christian family, right and wrong were very clear-cut. When I didn't live up to the standards of behaviour expected, I was wracked with guilt and shame. How are the aspirational mighty fallen! Doomed to failure because of wholly unrealistic expectations of being human! Today I recognize my reality to be more in keeping with the images in Brian McCabe's poem 'In the Skip'.

In the Skip
Half a dozen bricks
are clinging to their brickness
and to the idea of being
a wall.

Drawers lean on drawers as if
their crazy staircase could recall
the time it was a kitchen cabinet.

A mattress, doubled up, yearns
to yawn, stretch, turn over and
scratch itself where it's ripped.

Dust, yes there is dust.
And sometimes I think
my history is there in the skip:

a gap that was once for sitting on;
a piece missing its jigsaw;
a smatter of glass, convinced
it was always meant to be a window.

I peer into the rubble to see
what's salvageable.[1]

That's me, I thought, when I first came across the poem. The recognition was not negative. There was a freedom in it. To accept the mess is to be released from the oppression of never feeling 'good enough', and to open up the possibility of finding gifts in the gutter of my personal reality.

Over the years artists of all kinds, religious and non-religious, have been crucial to this process. They have cut through my defences, ignorance and self-deception in ways that rational argument often doesn't do. I have found liberation, not to say salvation, in their honesty. The writer Alexander Solzhenitsyn was right when he said that the purpose of art, of artists and writers, is to vanquish lies. It was a sculpture that first brought home powerfully to me the importance of getting in touch with the issues in myself I sought to deny.

Working with what is

Back in the late 1980s when I was training for ordination, one of our tutors showed us a picture of Brazilian sculptor Guido Rocha's *The Tortured Christ*. It is a disturbing piece with the Latin American crucified Christ screaming out in pain from his cross. Rocha depicted his own experience of torture in this figure. I couldn't take my eyes off it. I was struck by the hands of this Christ, the symbol of our deepest humanity, quite literally getting to grips with the nails, the symbols of our deepest inhumanity.

At the time, I was conscious of a long-standing difficult relationship with which I had never really come to terms. As a consequence the fallout of this unexamined experience kept intruding into my life in emotional reactions that were not proportionate with the present situation that had triggered them. Looking at Guido's Christ I realized at a level that went much deeper than rational assent that the only way to deal with brokenness and inhumanity was to get to grips with it, not deny it. Only then can we resurrect our lives from the body-blow experiences and emotional traumas that sometimes crucify and entomb us, limiting our capacity for joy and delight. Is it possible that part of the reason the messiness of human experience can be so debilitating is *not* because by nature that's necessarily how it must be, but because in the way we seek to deny or distance ourselves from it, to pretend that human reality is anything other than it is, it cannot be anything other than destructive?

Over the years I've learnt that the great scriptural stories of faith are not there to be believed in, but to be lived out. To see them as history is to limit their truth, to confine them to happening at one time and place. As Richard Rohr said of such stories, 'They are usually not historical fact, but invariably they are spiritual genius.'[2] More than history, they are your story and my story – true of human experience in all times and places. They come alive as we work with them in the light of our own life story. So let me tell you a little of mine as a way into the archetypal myth of Adam and Eve, which has much to say about what it means to be human.

I do not park on double-yellow lines. Quite rightly so, but neither will I stop on them, even briefly to drop off a passenger. Unless, of course, the person is disabled and I have a legitimate disabled badge to place on the dashboard. The discomfort I feel if asked to stop without the latter is a source of amusement for my husband Chris, and a reminder of a younger self who was so anxious to please and not to get into trouble. In all kinds of ways this 'Little Ruth' still makes her presence felt in my psyche. When I go against the grain of what is generally thought to be right I do so only if, after deep reflection, I think what I've been taught is wrong, or, if I am not thinking straight at all, my response is an aberration. To break consciously with a long-held code of conduct is far more costly for me than for someone who likes sailing close to the wind.

Luckily for me, and unluckily for 'Little Ruth', she is not a lone 'figure' in my emotional landscape. Her fear, and what I've come to see as her 'small town' mentality, exist uneasily in company with a wilder self who wants to live life to the full, unfettered by any fear (except that of living a 'little' life), and aware that living creatively inevitably involves taking risks. This deep engagement with life is captured in the beautifully tragic writing of Michael Ondaatje in *The English Patient*. Count László de Almásy, the patient of the title, tries to save the life of his lover, Katherine Clifton, after she is seriously injured in a plane crash. He goes to find help but by the time he returns she is dead.

And all the names of the tribes, the nomads of faith who walked in the monotone of the desert and saw brightness and faith and colour. The way a stone or found metal box or bone can become loved and turn eternal in a prayer. Such glory of this country she enters now and becomes part of. We die containing a richness of lovers and tribes, tastes we have swallowed, bodies we have plunged into and swum up as if rivers of wisdom, characters we have climbed into as if trees, fears we have hidden in as if caves. I wish for all this to be marked on my body when I am dead. I believe in such cartography – to be marked by nature, not just label ourselves on a map like the names of rich men and women on buildings. We are communal histories, communal books. We are not owned or monogamous in our taste or experience. All I desired was to walk upon such an earth that had no maps.

I carried Katherine Clifton into the desert, where there is the communal book of moonlight. We were among the rumour of wells. In the palace of winds.[3]

My wilder self cries out, 'Yes!' to the intensity, colour and depth of experience expressed in Ondaatje's words.

Knowledge and conflict

Between this passionate self and Little Ruth stands Eve – *Havva* in Hebrew, meaning 'life-giver' – reaching out for the apple in the garden of Eden in the second creation story of the Bible. She begins life with Adam in paradisal innocence. Eden is a place of pleasure not perfection. Perfection is an illusion. It does not exist because life is dynamic, while perfection has nowhere else to go. It is the destination reached, the goal attained. It might be argued that we are evolving towards perfection, but I don't think the evidence of evolution supports such a view. Human evolution is about surviving and flourishing, adapting to changing contexts, but not, on the evidence we have, moving towards a perfect state of being. This is more in keeping with St Augustine's redefinition of perfection as running rightly, not thinking you've arrived.

So Eden is not symbolic of a perfect state. It is a sanctuary providing protection, abundance and nurture. Eve and Adam are unselfconscious and at ease within its confines. All their needs are met, but Eve wants to learn more. Encouraged on by the serpent, she reaches out and eats the fruit from the Tree of the Knowledge of Good and Evil, not out of disobedience – how can one who has not eaten from the tree giving the knowledge of good and evil distinguish between right and wrong? – but because it is her nature to explore and to ask questions. When she and Adam eat the fruit their eyes are opened and they become self-consciously aware of their nakedness. This moment of insight seals their future, ultimately driving them from Eden into the barren lands beyond. According to one strand of Jewish tradition brought to my attention by my friend Rabbi Professor Jonathan Magonet, this story is the experience of every human being.

We begin life in innocence. For most of the world's population this state of security is all too short, with the reality of poverty, disease and other kinds of deprivation impinging even before the first breath is drawn. Even those of us who are luckier cannot remain forever in a state of innocence/ignorance. We are curious by nature and if we are to survive we need to understand the life into which we have been born. Eve, Adam and the serpent exist in each of us: Eve, the part reaching out for knowledge; the serpent, the impulse in us to explore; Adam, the inability to take responsibility for what we do, wanting to blame someone else when things go pear-shaped.

Knowledge opens up the world for us, but in so doing it also makes us vulnerable. We discover how much greater and more complicated is reality than in our innocence/ignorance we understood it to be. The loss of innocence, the acquiring of knowledge takes us into the unknown. The experience is exhilarating and life-enhancing but it will inevitably also lead us into seemingly barren places of uncertainty, conflict, doubt, challenge, failure, regret and grief. As Kahlil Gibran wrote in *The Prophet*, 'Your pain is the breaking of the shell that encloses your understanding.'[4]

This journey of discovery, of breaking out and growing up, connects us with our capacity for both glorious creativity and desperate destructiveness of the kind inaccessible in our earlier protected state of innocence. Reconciling these capacities is a lifelong task.

Questions

1 I spoke of 'Little Ruth' and a wilder self. Can you recognize and name the different 'voices' in your own psyche and note the tensions that may exist between them?

2 As your life experience and knowledge has developed, what have been the difficult issues of understanding for you?

2

Life after Eden

One day as part of my training for ordination I and my fellow ordinands were asked to think about what made us physically distinguishable from other people. Having answered that question we had to disguise ourselves so that we became unrecognizable. Once the disguise was complete we had to decorate it in a way that said as much as possible about how we understood ourselves at that point in time. Think *Blue Peter*, egg boxes, sticky-back plastic, tape, glue, cereal packets and paint and you'll be on the right lines. At the end of the exercise the room was awash with the detritus of would-be artists. Discarded ideas that hadn't worked littered the floor. The place looked as if a class of 5-year-olds had been let loose in it.

Creativity and mess

Being creative with the raw materials of our unfolding human experience and understanding can be just as messy, but clearing up the fallout is usually far more complicated than sweeping up the waste paper and craft materials remaining at the end of an art session. Once we have left its confines, the 'Eden' of innocence/ignorance is for ever closed to us. There's no going back. You can only relinquish unhelpful baggage and carry on the journey you've started. The rest of Scripture after Adam and Eve are cast out of Eden is the story of human beings struggling to live with their growing knowledge and their limitations of understanding in a complex and sometimes cruel world.

Understandably, some of us try to protect ourselves from the harsher realities of human experience by retreating into little 'Edens' of our own making, such as belief systems that offer security but don't stand up to searching questions from outsiders. These can be religious or secular. We stick with people who see things as we do, and denounce as damned or deluded those who question our position. That way we can dismiss them. My lovely sister-in-law Jan once belonged to a religious group called Abundant Life. It offered clear-cut certainty and expected its members to accept unquestioningly the beliefs it held. Jan's questing mind eventually took her out of the group. In family folklore it's now referred to as Abundant Strife, but at the time it gave her the security she needed. Even the most dedicated explorers among us have moments when we long for an easy, uncomplicated existence, and the innocence of past certainties fills us with poignant longing for what can no longer be.

I spoke earlier of Eve standing between Little Ruth and my wilder self. In seeking to reconcile these two drives, the activity of Eve was present in the questions I wanted answered: What does Little Ruth fear? Are her fears still justified? What makes relationships work? What are the different aspects that shape who we are and how we express that? To what extent can my wilder self live out her longing? What is the inherited wisdom about this, in my community and beyond it? Do I agree with it? If not, why not? How does my behaviour impact on others? Is the self something to be set aside as one makes space for others? And so on. What questions might the Eve of your own mind ask in the light of your life experience?

The rabbinic interpretation of the story of Adam and Eve to which Jonathan introduced me really rings true. The more I experience life, and the more I learn through reading, study and conversations with others whose experiences differ from my own, the more questions there are. My long-held truths are challenged by people I meet from different cultures, social backgrounds, religious persuasions and sexual identities. That's difficult when those 'truths' are important to my sense of identity. Challenges to rethink my understanding inevitably raise questions about who I am. I identify very much with Henrik Ibsen's words, 'To live is to war with trolls in the holds of the heart and mind,' but I've also learnt that the complexity, confusion and contradictory energies within me need not necessarily be a source of negative conflict. I know what Tennessee Williams was on about when he said, 'If I got rid of my demons, I'd lose my angels.'[1] In other words, what I wrestle with might also be what enables me to take wing.

I guess it's not surprising in the light of this that my own path drew me into working with people in the wider world living through conflict or its aftermath. I felt immense hope when I heard the stories of men and women who had got things badly wrong in their lives in violent situations and who, in dealing with the legacy of their deeds, had developed deep insight and searching compassion. Perhaps I recognized in their experience something of the shadow I struggled with in myself and eventually had to confront head-on.

At a time when deep grief and trauma in my life clouded my judgement and I made a complete fool of myself, hurting others in the process, I was sent the following poem written by Monica Furlong. It was a real lifesaver for me. I carried it everywhere and read it often.

A slum is where somebody else lives . . .
A slum is where somebody else lives,
Help is what others need.
We all want to be the priest, social worker, nurse
The nun in the white habit giving out the soup –
To work from a position of power,
The power being
That we are not the shuffler in the queue
Holding out his bowl.

But there is only one way into the kingdom
– To be found out in our poverty.
That is why the citizens are a job lot –
Unhappily married, the feckless mother of eight,
The harlot no longer young,
The lover of little girls, the sexually untameable,
The alcoholic, the violent, and those whose drink is despair.

Show me not, Lord, your rich men
With their proud boasts of poverty and celibacy,
They are too much for me.
Hide me from those who want to help
And still have strength to do so.
Only those who get on with their lives
And think they have nothing to give
Are any use to me.
Let your bankrupts feed me.[2]

I had discovered myself to be a 'shuffler in the queue'. Monica's poem suggested it was only in this poverty of spirit that a person might enter into the deeper experience described as 'the kingdom'. It gave me hope that, if I worked to understand what had happened, this painful setback might then become a step forward.

Later when I bought the book containing the poem, I realized the version I'd been sent had been edited. 'The lover of little girls . . .' had been omitted. Its presence in the original disturbed me, and remains disturbing. It would be much easier to take a black and white stance, to consider human beings to be either good or bad. That way we don't have to struggle with where to draw the line. It's clear-cut. We can try to convert those who have crossed it, or give up on them. They are beyond the pale, to be condemned, not considered 'like us' in any way. Such judgement often mirrors our response to our own faults and failings. We seek to distance ourselves as far from them as possible.

Not being honest – with ourselves if with no one else – makes it harder to deal with what is destructive in us and others. It also denies the insight of biblical stories in which the least reputable, most unexpected people are often the means of God's grace. Moses the murderer saves the Hebrew slaves. David the boy who floors Goliath goes on to become an adulterous king but is still revered by later generations. Elijah the great prophet misses God in the sound of silence. Ranting prophets reveal God's judgement and love. Ignorant and arrogant disciples are chosen by Jesus to live his Word. Outcasts from respectable religious circles become the company of Jesus and not, I think, simply because 'it is the sick who need a doctor', but because it is often broken people who know their own failure and inhumanity who can become a source of healing for others.

As I struggled to come to terms with the grief I felt and the knock-on effect of it on my sanity I was struck by an image from a parable I'd known since childhood but never really connected with before. It tells of a farmer sowing his seed. Some falls on rock where it cannot be sustained. Some falls among weeds that choke the new shoots. Other seeds fall into good soil and there's a rich harvest. At this low point in my life it suddenly struck me that 'good soil' is nothing more than muck and decomposing matter that when worked carefully becomes fertile compost in which good things can take root, grow and flourish.

This is profoundly encouraging to those of us who know how messy we are as human beings. Personal and professional experience has made me aware this is the reality for far more people than we might realize. Novelist Rachel Joyce captures it beautifully in *The Unlikely Pilgrimage of Harold Fry*. In retirement, Harold hears that a friend from years ago is dying of cancer. He sets off to post a letter to her but ends up walking all the way from Devon to Northumberland to see her. On the journey he meets and shares kindness with many people living lives more or less complicated than his own. During an unexpected conversation in a station cafe with an elegantly dressed, silver-haired stranger, Harold realizes his companion is nothing like he first imagined:

> He was a chap like himself, with a unique pain; and yet there would be no knowing that if you passed him in the street, or sat opposite him in a café and did not share his teacake. Harold pictured the gentleman on a station platform, smart in his suit, looking no different from anyone else. It must be the same all over England. People were buying milk, or filling cars with petrol, or even posting letters. And what no one else knew was the appalling weight of the thing they were carrying inside. The superhuman effort it took sometimes to be normal, and a part of things that appeared easy and everyday. The loneliness of that.[3]

When I wrote the first draft of this book I asked a much respected colleague to be the 'reader-over-my-shoulder'. We met up after he'd read the Introduction and first few chapters. At the end he said he'd like me to see a picture in his living room. It was an etching, a self-portrait by the artist Celia Paul. It shows her enlightened left side as clearly defined and light-filled, but this clarity and light darkens into a right side that is not a side at all because her now featureless darkness is either boundless or indistinct from a greater darkness. Seeing the etching was like looking in a mirror. It was both shocking and comforting; shocking to be confronted with uncomfortable realities and comforting to discover another person recognizing this reality with all its inherent problems and possibilities.

Not only do artists have the capacity to reveal reality to us, they can also give us ideas about how we might live that reality creatively. It's no coincidence I suspect that I'm drawn to the work of artists who make wonderful things out of rubbish. The Japanese sculptor Sayaka Ganz takes my breath away with dynamic animals made from plastic utensils reclaimed from the dump.[4] One of my favourites is on the cover of this book. Sayaka's sculptures capture what I have experienced to be true of human beings as well.

Through my work I've met many people consigned to the human scrap heap who, with intense, disciplined and costly work, have reclaimed their lives and very often contributed far more to the good of the world than those who have condemned them. Some of my greatest teachers and dearest friends are people who have done terrible things, or who, alongside acts of great compassion, wrestle with personal demons that at times have caused suffering to others and themselves. In their lives, as with Celia Paul's etching, I see reflections of my own.

Questions

1 In what ways do you try to protect yourself from knowledge and experience that is hard to handle?
2 How have difficult experiences shaped for the better the person you are today?
3 What kind of safe 'space' do you need when you are dealing with difficult truths about yourself? Do you offer that kind of space to others in similar circumstances?

3

Tools for the journey

If you recognize anything of your own experience in what I've written so far the question becomes where do we go from here? I want to highlight five capacities I think are helpful, even essential tools for tackling the reality I've described.

Risk-taking

By risk-taking I mean being prepared to step beyond what we know in order to be open to what we have yet to learn. The story of Adam and Eve makes it clear that growing in knowledge and understanding inevitably takes us out of our comfort zone. In the comprehensive school where I worked as chaplain, the children talk about being 'in the pit'. This is the point when they understand nothing of what's being taught, when they're wrestling with difficult new ideas, may well want to give up, and feel really stupid. If they stick with the task they eventually come out of the pit and experience one of those wonderful 'Ah, yes!' moments when the light finally dawns and they have a real sense of achievement. Maggie, one of their fantastic Maths teachers, encourages her students to recognize these times of being 'in the pit' as a normal part of the process of learning. To learn is to be prepared to take the risk of looking stupid, being confused, getting things wrong and missing the point entirely. That may not feel great as a student in class learning geometry, but the consequences are nothing compared to what might happen if we're 'in the pit' trying to make sense of human relationships, moral and ethical dilemmas, and all the aspects of being human that are not as clear-cut and formulaic as a mathematical equation. I spoke earlier about the pitfalls of working with the many shades of who we are. When we find ourselves in a hole, the shame, distress and sense of being out of control can be crippling not only to us but to others in the fallout zone.

The collection of myths, law codes, poems, songs, sayings, prophecies and communal stories/histories that make up the Hebrew Scriptures expresses profoundly the struggles of human beings to understand and work with this reality, its tragedies and triumphs. Inherent in the collection are contradictions, arguments and counter-arguments, pictures of human beings in all their complexity and expressions of human emotion from the heights of ecstasy to the depths of human depravity. The book of Job, for example, struggled with the question of why blameless people suffered. It did not share the Deuteronomic belief expressed in other biblical books that if you lived a blameless life you would not suffer.

In my younger days I was critical of the Old Testament for its portrayal of clearly flawed human beings and pictures of a God who seemed to exhibit on a grand scale the worst human traits. As I've confronted my own inhumanity I've found much comfort in Holy Scriptures that make a point of holding the human condition in all its many shades. These texts invite us into ongoing dialogue.

Like the people of the Bible, I inhabit a religious tradition rooted in a dynamic conversation between inherited Scripture, experience and ritual practice. Its coherence lies primarily in it being practised as opposed to proclaimed, and in changing as new insights and experiences come to bear upon it. To be unchanging is not to remain the same, for if I and my faith remain static in a world that is evolving around me, I and my faith are no longer what they were. Revelation is therefore not a one-off set in stone, but an ongoing process of discovery.

The truth of new understanding may not be immediately obvious to us. We need to 'get to grips' with it. In the Hebrew Scriptures when Jacob was on the long road to redressing the wrong he had done to his brother Esau, he spent a night wrestling at the Ford of Jabbok with a character who might be a man or might be an angel. His identity is unclear. The man/angel leaves Jacob with a dislocated thigh. In the encounter Jacob learns some important lessons, but what is revealed does not come without conflict and pain. Risk-taking, and the conflict that comes with what risk-taking may reveal, is part of life if we are to grow and develop to our fullest potential.

In the present age we have come to value in the West a rather mechanistic view of the Cosmos. There is a sense that if we work out how all the 'bits' work, and put together these pieces of knowledge, we will have sussed reality. Away with myths and metaphors! We have come of age and put away childish things. Yet in so doing we are also in danger of throwing away the baby with the bath water. In his wonderful book *The Master and His Emissary*,[1] Iain McGilchrist explores the most recent research in the field of neuroscience. He dispels the popular misconception about the two hemispheres of the brain dealing with different aspects of human functioning. What is different is the priority of each hemisphere, the focus of its attention. Thus the left hemisphere has a narrow focus and is engaged by the mechanical and non-living. It processes primary experience and detail. It provides labels, concepts and 'maps' that enable us to navigate the world around us. It doesn't have the big picture, and putting together the 'bits' of information it processes does not give it the big picture.

The right hemisphere has the bigger picture. It sees context, is engaged by the living, sees connections that enable it to encounter the world and develop relationships. It understands things that flow, like time and music. It sees visual depth, has perspective and recognizes dimension. It understands the power of metaphor and myth. It experiences what is present. The left hemisphere can only process the primary experiences that it is given access to by the right hemisphere and create representations. By the nature of its attention the left hemisphere doesn't know what it doesn't know because it operates in neat systems and can't see outside them. McGilchrist argues that we live in a time and society in which the priorities of the left hemisphere dominate. This becomes apparent in destructive perfectionism, unrealistic expectations, black and white thinking that lacks subtlety and nuance, competitiveness, abstracted thinking, a world-view that sees problems as the result of other people's failings, a 2-D existence represented on screens, rather than lived out in the flesh. Do you recognize that reality?

I have probably done a great disservice to McGilchrist's work by trying to capture a little of its flavour in so few words, but what is important to me about his research and reflection is the idea that there is more to reality than we can pin down. We need art, music, poetry, myths and metaphors to give expression to the experiences that don't fit neat formulae. However great we think our knowledge, we have so much more to learn. As a teenager I thought I knew it all. The older I get the more I realize I don't know or understand. As James Hollis puts it, 'The world is more magical, less predictable, more autonomous, less controllable, more varied, less simple, more infinite, less knowable, more wonderfully troubling than we could have imagined being able to tolerate when we were young.'[2]

Respect

Since we do not know everything, or even a small fraction of everything, the decisions we make on the basis of what we, and the communities to which we belong, understand may not always be right. Being attentive to the wisdom of the past is important, but not all the wisdom of what's gone before remains relevant. The people of the Bible, for example, did not have the scientific understanding we have today. Their medical knowledge was primitive compared to what we know now. The limitations with which they worked differ from many of those we confront.

This means that the way they understood their communities, and the rules they lived by, cannot be set in stone for generations whose understanding and experience of life is so utterly different.

Please note, 'different' does not necessarily mean 'more advanced'. Scientifically and technologically superior we may be, but we are as capable of inhumanity as our predecessors, and have much greater capacity to destroy life than did our ancestors. Nevertheless it is our responsibility, individually and collectively, to respect and work with the wisdom we have inherited and to revise, reshape or add to it when it ceases to speak into the heart and mind of our own experience. This can only be done respectfully, because respect takes seriously what is addressed. Respect enables us to connect with the issues, rather than remain aloof from them. In this way we have the opportunity to gain a better understanding. A respectful relationship enables questions to be asked that would otherwise be deemed inappropriate or dismissed without thought.

Recently I was invited to attend a meeting between English Defence League leaders and a group of Muslims. Despite major differences of opinion and experience they took time to listen to one another. They discovered shared fears and concerns. They were able to engage with the humanity of the other. The conversation challenged assumptions on both sides. It wasn't always easy but by the end of the day those present were keen the conversation should continue. Respect also means accepting the possibility that in the conversation our own views may be challenged and changed by what is said.

The meeting I attended stands in sharp contrast to debates set up on television news programmes. Sometimes it seems those asked to participate are chosen because they have polar opposite opinions, and are geared to diatribe not dialogue. 'Good' television struggles to include conversations in which people who are very different speak and listen to one another in order to develop understanding. In society more generally, where are the respectful, safe places of this kind where we can ask the difficult questions about the complexity of our experience?

Respect does not mean agreeing with the perspective of another person. How can I respect you if you have caused harm to me or my family? Respect in this context is about accepting that, like me, you have a life history to share that may help me understand why you stand where you do. The reasons for your position may be positive and negative, as is the case for mine too. If I respect you enough to allow you to tell your story, and you respect me enough to allow me to tell you mine, it's possible that we will both emerge with greater understanding, not only of one another but of what it means to be human.

Regret

Life is complicated. Because of our limitations we will inevitably fail, fall short, screw up and fall down. Working with reality therefore requires a certain amount of humility and a great deal of honesty about who we are. Perhaps the most any of us can hope to be is a half-decent human being. With this in mind I'm drawn very much to the suggestion of the then Archbishop of Canterbury, Rowan Williams, that 'ethics is essentially about how we navigate our own and other people's vulnerabilities'.[3]

Understood in this light, ethics loses the flavour it sometimes has of the enlightened few imposing impossibly difficult codes of behaviour on more fallible human beings. It becomes instead a collaborative endeavour of people who are all too conscious of their human fragilities and are seeking shared guidelines that help one another to own and work with these vulnerabilities in a way that is life-enhancing rather than death-dealing.

To work with our vulnerabilities we need to accept they exist. To accept what is hard to accept we need safe spaces. I don't know about you but when I've got things wrong what I need is the help of someone who will not condemn me. Condemnation only causes me to close down and cut off. Only in the acceptance of another wise friend am I able to look at what I've done and sort out how to work with what's happened. Into this mix comes the experience of regret.

Regret is usually seen as a negative emotion. To regret nothing has great appeal, but although regret is not a comfortable response, its presence can signify something positive. I'm not talking here about regret experienced for choices *not* made and actions *not* taken. I'm referring to the regret that comes when one's chosen course causes pain and suffering, either personally or to other people. Regret indicates that the regretful one cares about the impact of their decisions on other people and themselves. For the most part I do not think most of us make the mistakes we make and get into the mess we get into because we want to hurt those who get hurt by our choices.

Regret is often the experience of those who haven't played safe and who have run with a situation, perhaps in part to try and understand better others or themselves or the life they're leading. Playing safe is a sure way of staying simple, but given that we don't know everything, we're bound to get things wrong. Sometimes we need to make our own mistakes to see why a particular course of action is not a good idea. Sometimes our course of action may be right, but if it is out of kilter with the accepted norms of our community then we or others may be hurt. Peacemakers often find themselves in this position. Their work requires they have contact with the community with whom they are in conflict. Members of their own community may well see this contact as betrayal, even treason: 'You're talking with the people responsible for my husband's death. How can you betray his memory?'

This simple example also shows how difficult it may be to determine the 'right' thing. What do we mean by the word 'right'? Right for whom? Right at what level and in what context? For example, deep, genuine and passionate love between two people is a wonderful and 'right' thing, unless one or both is married to someone else. The love may be the same, but other factors like commitment, trust, loyalty and duty enter the equation.

Reconciliation

We do not live in an ideal world where everything falls into place neatly and is life-givingly right at every level. We do not always have a clear choice between right and wrong, good and bad, even when we are clear about what those terms mean. The fallout from poor decisions may be much greater than we could have anticipated in advance. A major element of emotional maturity is being able to reconcile creatively the tensions that threaten to tear us apart.

Generally reconciliation is something associated with the aftermath of conflict, but all of us on a daily basis must try to reconcile competing demands upon our lives. Couples grapple with their work–life balance, particularly when they have children. Who is going to do what and when? How can the different demands of partnership, parenting and professional life be held together healthily? Can my aspirations as an individual be reconciled with what actually is, or is significant change demanded and, if so, am I capable of it?

Back in the 1950s, Mr Universe, Steve Reeves, played Hercules in the major box-office success of the same name. In the film, Hercules is captured by his enemies and tied between two teams of horses, one black, the other white. These teams are sent off in opposite directions with the intention of tearing Hercules apart. Being Hercules, he manages under great duress to hold them together and survive. Holding together the tensions that threaten to tear us apart today also requires Herculean effort at times. Sometimes, for all kinds of reasons, we just don't have it in us and our lives are torn apart. If and how we put them back together again depends very much upon the type of person we are, what has happened and how the people involved regard fallibility and failure.

Resilience

Reconciling the conflicting demands within us, and between ourselves and others demands great energy. Reconciliation may not be something that happens easily or quickly. Some situations are not reconcilable and the consequences of choices made must be lived with, rather than lived beyond. Those who have had their hearts broken by someone loved and trusted will know the deep scars that can be left. Sometimes families fall apart and restoration isn't possible. Difficult experiences at work leave their mark. Disputes with neighbours provoke bad feeling that rankles on. Things happen over which we have no control – illness, tragedy, disaster – and we must find ways of living with the aftermath. 'I'm never going to let myself be in that situation again', becomes our cry, although we may not always be in a position to prevent that.

Resilience is sometimes hard-won through deep grief, disappointment and despair. Each loss, each setback, each hard knock offers the opportunity for us to develop greater resilience. By resilience I mean the capacity to deal with adversity rather than be destroyed by it. A good example of this might be the people of Garbage City on the edge of Cairo in Egypt.

In the recent past the garbage-collectors of Cairo lived, quite literally, on top of the garbage heap that amassed near the pyramids in Giza. The site wasn't great for tourism so the garbage-collecting community was moved into the desert on the edge of another side of Cairo. Apart from destitution, where else is there to go for such people? Well, the only way was up. Bringing back the detritus of Cairo, the garbage-collectors and their families meticulously sorted through the rubbish, recycling everything recyclable. They risked disease and injury but over time they were able to build brick homes until they had created what is now known as Garbage City. Packs of sorted plastic, cardboard and metal are piled high in the narrow streets. Looking down on the city from the cliff that forms its backdrop, the roofs of some blocks run deep in tin cans. It is an extraordinary place of industry. To not only survive but to make a living from rubbish in this place is an act of extraordinary resilience.

The people of Garbage City have developed resilience under duress, but it's also helpful to have psychologically safe spaces in which we can work with the difficult aspects of our experience without fear and external pressure. I need the support and wisdom of others who understand their own darkness and can help me work with mine from a place of compassion not from a position of misguided self-righteous judgement. Compassion – that word again! So easily spoken and so hard to live, even when we recognize just how crucial it is. So let's now look at specific areas of human life and explore the complexity and questions that are part of them. In Chapter 4 I'll look at the difficulties of living with other people. Before we move on, here are some questions to recap what we've been exploring in Part 1.

Questions

1 How has your past shaped your present perceptions?
2 What are the aspects of being human you struggle with today?
3 How open are you to new knowledge and experience?
4 How do you respond to people whose understanding is very different from your own?
5 What qualities do you have to help you live with complexity?

Part 2

COMMUNITY

4

No man is an island

———————•◆•———————

'I don't know how to answer your question because I don't exist.'

The woman is speaking to me quietly and thoughtfully through a translator. Her words capture the essence of sentiments expressed by others in the room. I am in the Democratic Republic of the Congo working with a group of survivors of sexual violence. Some have been raped many times. Some bear physical scars of unspeakable violation. Some are suicidal. All have one child or more as a result of rape. All were thrown out of their homes and communities when they became pregnant through the sexual abuse. The rapists – militiamen, relatives, professionals and opportunists – go unpunished. Not only must these women and girls deal with the trauma of being raped, becoming pregnant and giving birth, usually without medical help, they must also cope with the homelessness and destitution that comes as a result of being rejected by their families because of these experiences. I wonder at a community so brutalized by war and poverty, that the innocent pay such a price and the guilty walk free.

Lest this provoke an unwarranted bout of self-righteous horror at the failings of another community that is 'not like us', I note that around the time I went to the Congo the BBC, along with other news media, highlighted a report by HM Inspectorate of Constabulary. It indicated that the response of police to domestic abuse in England and Wales was alarming and ineffective, and put thousands of people at risk from harm or even murder.

I've heard of another community in the developing world whose compassionate response to the shortcomings of its people challenges me in a different way. When one of their number does something wrong that person is made to stand in the centre of the village. They remain there until all the other members of the community have come by to tell them everything they think is *good* about them. They are not defined by what they get wrong, but by what they get right and the qualities they have. Their place and value in the community is emphasized with the expectation that this experience of belonging and of being affirmed will put right the sense of alienation and unhappiness that prompted their antisocial action.

Being community – for good or ill?

In a nutshell these two uncommon stories capture the death-dealing and the life-giving potential of community life and the ability of communities to abuse or build up their members. My childhood and Christian faith have taught me to see the concept of community as central to human well-being but my experience has also taught me that communities can be claustrophobic and crippling in their demands for conformity to their particular codes of conduct.

An episode from my childhood comes to mind. My cousin was getting married and I needed to make an outfit for myself. I longed for stylish elegance but for whatever reason ended up making a brown skirt and brown waistcoat that were so unlike me in colour and design I still remember the deep embarrassment I felt wearing them to the wedding. That experience summed up all the restrictions of life I associated with being 'small town', as I called it.

At the beginning of Chapter 2 I spoke about the exercise I and my ordinand friends had to do, disguising our obvious characteristics and then, on top of the disguise, illustrating who we understood ourselves to be. As part of the latter I cut a slit in the white card I'd used to cover my torso. Behind it, on a toilet roll tube, I had wound strands of multi-coloured paper, the tips of which protruded through the slit with a 3-inch cut-out girl standing with her arms raised. At the appropriate point in our group discussion I pulled out this little girl on her umbilical cord of string, along with all the coloured strands, so that they fell like a rainbow from my stomach to the floor. Looking back I realize how this was a key, and at the time largely unconscious, attempt to unearth the vital me that had become lost in the brown 'oughts' and 'shoulds' and 'have-tos' that masked my true colours.

The adolescent me who railed against 'brown and dowdy' was beginning to wrestle with the community values in which I'd been raised and to question the identity I had taken upon myself in my family. Archbishop Desmond Tutu wrote:

> None of us comes into the world fully formed. We would not know how to think, or walk, or speak, or behave as human beings unless we learned it from other human beings. We need other human beings in order to be human. I am because other people are. A person is entitled to a stable community life, and the first of these communities is the family.[1]

Through the dependency of childhood we learn from key people in our lives who we are, or who they think we should be, and what is expected of us. The influence will, to varying degrees, be a mix of

26

positive and negative since families are never perfect and some are less perfect than others. As we grow up and begin to experience wider life, we may have a sense of ourselves as other than we had understood to that point. This may put us in conflict with the community of which we've felt very much a part. If a community functions well it enables its members to continue to grow and develop with the logical expectation that they may reach a point when they need to move on into a different type of communal space. This is to be celebrated, but all too often those remaining in the community see the departure of other members as negative. Until more recently, for example, when those who tested out their vocation in religious orders decided at some point to leave, their departure was taken as a betrayal, or a sign that somehow the departing ex-novice was not up to the demands of community life. They were ushered unceremoniously out of the back door, often without the opportunity to say goodbye to those with whom they'd become friends.

Orthodoxy vs orthopraxis

As Desmond Tutu indicates, we need other people in order to have some sense of who we are, but who we are as individuals can put us at odds with the wider communal identity. In part the problem seems to be seeing community as a concrete, fixed reality, rather than an ever-changing 'organism' that is shaped by its members as much as it shapes them. The tragedy of communities is when their identity becomes fixed and the life within them is suffocated; when they get caught up in the rules of the community and the rightness of its beliefs about life (orthodoxy) rather than prioritizing right ways of being (orthopraxis).

Instead of enabling members to live and thrive in the world, they may become 'safe' havens from it, thus requiring the psychological doors of the community to be barred and the windows to be barricaded against outside influences. Some Christian communities, for example, justify this latter approach by quoting Gospel texts like John 15.19, to indicate that they are in the world but not of it and therefore don't need to engage with it. In contrast Jesus was constantly taking his disciples out of their comfort zone into places they would not otherwise have visited, to encounter people they distrusted or hated and to learn from them.

This is not to say that we do not need communal resting places and havens along the way of our lives, but the purpose of these is to help us engage with and live in the world, not retreat from it. One means of retreat from the world is by mentally living in the past.

The 'good old days'

Many people who have lived a long time, particularly through the Second World War, will bewail the fact that community life in the UK is not like it used to be. When they were young, they say, everyone knew everyone else in the community, and they all looked out for one another. Not like today when no one cares about their neighbour and we interact more with our smart device screens than face to face with flesh and blood humanity. I'm sure this is true, but it's not the whole truth.

It's convenient to forget that when my mum was a child the gulf between rich and poor was immense and those living in slums knew poverty in far more extreme ways than is generally the case in Britain today. There was no NHS. Treatment for illness depended upon what you could afford or the charity of others. Maternal and neonatal mortality rates were disturbingly high. Women were still in the early stages of securing equal opportunities and, oh yes, we were fighting a world war. I'm reminded of Victoria Wood's wonderful sketch in which she and Julie Walters play two cockney women digging away in the rubble after a night of German bombing, and talking indomitably about looking for the Christmas pudding, undaunted by the destruction around them: 'And if I find my husband as well, that's all to the good.'

Close-knit communities existed in a society of extreme inequalities where most people knew and accepted their place. Limitations of travel and opportunities for recreation meant that people lived for generations in the same place and made their own entertainment. Inevitably they would have known one another better and had more connections within their well-defined and usually monochrome neighbourhood. They were less welcoming and inclusive when in 1948, for example, 493 Jamaicans arrived on the *Empire Windrush* in Tilbury Docks wanting to make a new life here. For many locals the new arrivals were a 'difference' too far. *'They' were not of our own kind. How could they be like us? They were black.*

Community based on uniformity

The cracks in the idea that in the good old days our parents and grandparents knew how to be community became much more visible when what people were used to, the status quo, began to be challenged, when new people and new ideas began to seep into old, established communities. My grandparents could not have imagined the mix of ethnicities among the children in our local comprehensive school today, nor the fact that for the majority of students the colour of their peers is simply not an issue. They'd be startled, too, by the degree of religious plurality, the existence of militant atheism, the greater acceptance of differing sexualities, and female leadership in professions once the preserve of men.

The perfect present?

If the 'good old days' were not all they were cracked up to be, the present has its own problems, for all the advances in science and technology. We still wrestle today with what it means to be community and the degree to which it can be inclusive of diversity.

Internet technology (IT) has opened up the world for us. All kinds of communities are now available to us. Although IT has given us global access, I wonder how many of us use it to connect with people who are just like us, in our politics, interests or personalities, thus replicating the pattern of our forebears in choosing to connect with our own kind.

In recent years the rise in popularity of the far-right political parties suggests that however global our society has become there are a significant minority of people who either want to throw out 'foreigners' or strictly limit immigration in the UK. More mainstream political groups are also wrestling with the latter, as the impact of immigration on infrastructure creates increasing tension in local communities, particularly around housing priorities and work opportunities. *They – the immigrants – get housing while we are stuck on housing lists. They're taking our jobs. They're benefiting from our NHS without contributing to the cost of its existence . . .* and so on. The truth, or otherwise, of these claims seems to matter little to some who speak out one way or another. They feed, or do not take seriously, the deep-seated fears and beliefs regardless of the facts.

In March 2014 the UN Intergovernmental Panel on Climate Change (IPCC) produced its second report of a series, stating the impacts of global warming are likely to be 'severe, pervasive and irreversible', increasing tensions around migration, and, in the face of food, water and fuel shortages, threatening national security and increasing the risk of conflict.

My experience is that when communities feel secure they are much more open to different perspectives and patterns of living. When their well-being and identity feel under threat, they tend to retreat into the familiar and hunker down in the trenches of what always has been.

Questions

1 What did you learn about your identity as an individual from the communities of which you were a part during your 'growing-up years'?
2 Is the person others think you to be, the person you are?
3 What communities are important to you today?

5

Community challenge

If the past wasn't all it is sometimes cracked up to be and the present has its own fair share of problems, then as far as community is concerned things are pretty much as they always have been: messy and complicated. That's because community life wrestles with many tensions. I'm going to use my experience of different communities to illustrate some of the issues.

A person is a person through other persons

I am arguing with my brother. I'm eight years old. He is ten. The cause of our argument escapes me now. All I remember is that at some point he slaps me round the face. As an attentive child of Sunday school I decide not to rise to the attack. I am mindful of the words of Jesus in Luke's and Matthew's Gospels, 'To him who strikes you on the cheek, offer the other also . . .' I do just that and my brother takes great delight in slapping that one too! I am outraged that he isn't playing by the book. The smugness I felt in living out the words of Jesus is swiped from my face. *This isn't how it's supposed to be.* Not for the last time my naive and romantic take on religion is found wanting in the face of real life, and my sense of who I am and what I'm worth is called into question.

In the rough and tumble of family life I worked out my place in the general scheme of things, what worked or didn't work in dealing with other people, and why it was important to care for the needs of others outside my family. I knew where I belonged. For the most part I was confident in my identity and abilities.

My mother, in particular, was very community-minded. She was, and remains, the epitome of the good neighbour, caring for people living around her, pulling her weight, taking responsibility for the donkey-work that needs to happen if there is to be such a thing as community life. She was forever baking cakes for this or that event. When our garden produced more vegetables and fruit than we as a family needed, she gave away the excess to neighbours and those she knew were in need. Elderly friends received bouquets of lilac or sweet peas, roses or daffodils when the garden was abundantly in flower. She had four children going through the cubs, brownies, guides and scouts, so she became a guide leader, giving back service in response to all we had received in those organizations. Most particularly, life centred on the local church – middle-of-the-road Anglican – with its cycle of liturgical seasons, summer fetes, Christmas bazaars, jumble sales, concerts and community care. None of this was done with a fanfare of trumpets. She just quietly got on with it because that's what she'd been brought up to do.

No community is made up simply of the members it has at any one time. All the key people who have gone before in the lives of its present members live on in their patterns, for good or ill, or in their decisions to do things differently than was done to them. My mother's inherited commitment to the community was good. My sense that love was conditional upon me conforming to the family rules was not so good. When I got things wrong I was overwhelmed by the fear of rejection and feelings of guilt and shame that made me cautious about taking the kind of risks we need to take if we're to learn and grow.

As children we benefited from being part of a small market town community. It was safe, nurturing and 'known'. I had my place in the local scheme of things. I belonged. What was right and what was wrong was clear-cut. There were bad people and good people. Like any person I got things wrong, but I wasn't bad like the boys on the riot lines in Northern Ireland I watched on our black and white television, hurtling petrol bombs at one another or the soldiers on patrol. I wasn't bad like the very occasional girl in school who rumour had it was pregnant, and who disappeared from the playground. I wasn't suspect like the people who were not like us, people who were not white, middle-class, churchgoing folk. Not that I would have put it like that, if I thought about it much at all, but looking back I'm conscious that the prejudices I held, often completely unconsciously, were about people who were not like me and my community. To discover where we belong is as much a discovery about where we don't belong and about who we are not like, even if we've never met them to test out our assumptions about them.

Branching out

When I left home and moved to central London, living in a nurses' home opposite Big Ben on the corner of Westminster Bridge, I assumed I would be moving into a working community of people just like me. The reality was a wonderful and sometimes disturbing awakening to a much bigger world than the one with which I'd been familiar.

Nursing confronted me with people from all walks of life about whom I'd been able to hold very black and white views until that point. Homeless men and women who taught me that 'there but for the grace of God go I'. Drug addicts who'd fallen into drug-taking to escape awful family lives. 'Working-class' men and women who shared far more of what they had than many other people who possessed plenty. People of other cultures and faiths with whom I found I had much in common. Those I had easily condemned in the absence of experience became flesh and blood human beings, many of whom I enjoyed meeting. My world opened up and by and large I loved that.

I'm conscious now that this sudden engagement with human beings who were not like me, and with situations unlike anything I'd encountered before, happened in a reasonably controlled environment where my personal thoughts and feelings were able to adapt in a manageable way.

Alongside this, after something of a church crawl, I ended up in a falling-down Anglo-Catholic-with-a-sense-of-humour church in the Elephant and Castle, made up for the most part of south Londoners from the local high-rise housing estates, together with a smattering of middle-class professionals with a strong sense of social justice. We were gay and straight, black and white, broken, battered, beautiful people. In this community I learnt so much about generosity.

Many of the congregation had little in the way of material wealth, but what they had they shared. They were generous in spirit as well, slow to judge and condemn others, hospitable to all-comers, salt of the earth folk who brought out good flavours in humanity and didn't leave a bitter aftertaste. In their company I was able to ask the questions that began to tumble out as my childhood experience was challenged by my new life in London and the people I was meeting. I could no longer say that homosexuality was wrong. I could no longer say that homeless people ended up on the street through their own fault. I could no longer say the Bible was literally true, and that I knew exactly what God did or did not want of 'His' people. I could say that it is not acceptable to judge a person by the labels we give to one another and that everyone has a story to tell which reveals why they are how they are. I realized that if I had been through the experiences they had endured, I might well react as they had done. It was not that I was better than them, just luckier in the parents I'd been born to and the place I'd been raised.

I am hard-pushed to think of any community since my time at St Matthew's in the Elephant and Castle that has meant so much to me. When Chris and I married there, the congregation provided a bring-and-share lunch. Everyone was invited, along with family and friends from other places. If I tried to define what made this community such a great one to be part of, it is that it was secure in its own identity and therefore open to other identities in the wider community. It saw itself as a community on a journey of discovery, not one that had reached its destination. This meant it didn't have, and didn't need to have, all the answers, but was engaged in exploration. It wasn't interested in power politics, but in empowering the disparate people who were drawn in, as was I, by the unconditional warmth of its welcome. St Matthew's psychological roof was secure and the floor solid, so to speak, so its walls were permeable to all-comers, allowing people the freedom to come and go. It was prepared to wrestle with complexity and uncomfortable challenging truth. It lived out a commitment to the poor and oppressed, not only at a safe arm's length away, but right in our midst, so 'they' were no longer the anonymous 'poor and oppressed', but people with names, faces and compelling human stories. I refer to the church as 'it', but this 'it' was fleshed out in the diverse humanity of those who comprised the congregation.

Lest this sound cosy and romantic let me say that while St Matthew's was full of celebration, the commitment to service was emotionally costly, and working with the complexity of human experience that existed within and beyond our congregation was often messy, and did not always end happily. Sometimes life is 'shit' and there are no simple solutions. You can only support people as they live through the pain to whatever conclusion may be inevitable.

In 'the Elephant' I discovered and was encouraged to use gifts that had not been encouraged in my earlier life because I was focused on other priorities. I had my limits but I was learning there was a whole new world waiting to be discovered and that diversity wasn't something to be feared. I could also be part of the change demanded by the inhuman and inhumane elements of our collective experience. After four years of nursing training and being part of a community that had helped open my eyes I was ready for a life of further adventure, exploration and discovery.

Not belonging

I was not ready for the implosion of my world and seven years of 'wandering in the wilderness' wondering who I was and what life was really about, which was my actual experience. Disaster was what happened to other people, not to me.

My fiancé Chris's first curacy did not work well. Unemployment and homelessness seemed to be on the cards. For the first time in my life I experienced church leaders abusing their power. Perhaps a legacy of that experience is that I hate hierarchies, preferring to work collaboratively with others while being my own 'boss'. When power issues become part of a community's profile, pain often enters the equation with the abuse of power of which every human being is capable.

Thankfully, our situation was eventually vindicated by a more senior bishop and Chris was appointed to a new curacy in a semi-rural team of churches in Shropshire. As his wife, all my plans for further training in London and an adventurous life in the city or in foreign climes was abruptly put on hold as we headed for the Welsh borders and a very different community.

An essential element of good community is the sense of belonging. I did not belong in the new parish. I felt like a fish out of water. The people were lovely. The three villages were lovely. In many ways the ethos was not dissimilar to that of my childhood home, but I no longer belonged there. Moving to London I had discovered a love of city living and 'rock-face' work, and a spiritual home in St Matthew's. The traditional conservatism of the local churches, with PCCs arguing over issues that seemed to me to be trivial in the general scheme of things, left me feeling very much an outsider.

At that time there were no oncology courses available in the area, so I trained instead as a midwife. Apart from working on a labour ward and in the community, I found much of the work humdrum, and it took a while to break through the hostility of some of the qualified midwives who, I later learnt, were determined to hate me because I had trained at St Thomas's Hospital. It's interesting how my 'label' went before me and determined how people would treat me before they'd even met me. Apparently others had come before me and thrown their weight around a bit, critical of the care they saw being given in this county hospital. For some weeks I was held at arms' length because, surely, coming from the same place, I must be the same as my predecessors.

The impact of the past on the present

Although I managed to break through the initial hostility, the experience contributed to my sense that I was 'out of sorts' in this setting. Unexpectedly, I was also struggling to come to terms with the impact of Chris's experience in his first curacy, which had caused me to question the values of my family and the legitimacy of the Church. This turbulence took me by surprise because I had imagined that once we were out of the awful situation all would be well. I found, instead, that once the pressure was off and all was indeed well for Chris in his new place, reactions I had held at bay in order to deal with what was happening suddenly came to the fore. Each of us brings into the communities we join the legacy of the communities to which we've belonged, for good or ill.

As a recently married woman I was also finding that living in close relationship with Chris sometimes provoked strange reactions in me. These responses were disproportionate to things he said or did. Only in hindsight could I recognize my over-reaction, and wonder where it came from. In retrospect I suspect that the way Chris loved me made me feel safe enough to allow to the surface reactions and unresolved issues that I had learnt to repress when I was younger for fear of not being loved. Because the issues had not been dealt with, and I had not had the opportunity to learn how to manage the conflicting emotions of which we're all capable, they were now making themselves apparent in ways that were inconsistent with the maturity and insight I had developed in other areas of my understanding.

When we join new communities, we do not leave behind our past relationships and younger selves. The number of people you see in a community are but a fraction of the number of people who influence its life, whether or not they are still alive and physically present.

In general I think the ideal would be to live in communities where we feel we belong, but the seven years I lived like a fish out of water in rural contexts taught me much about who I was and who I was not – things that would not have become as starkly apparent had I been in a 'me-shaped' space. I did not feel at home, but I did begin to learn how to be more adaptable and to cope with circumstances that were not ideal. I would not have had my childhood any other way but I realize its security had not equipped me to deal well with insecurity.

How we experience a community may say as much, if not more, about who we are than about the merits of a particular community. If the resonances our inner landscape seeks in our external setting are absent, it doesn't matter how beautiful the outer reality is, we will not feel at home. I've subsequently discovered that I need the mix of city life and wild, windswept seascapes with mountains as the backdrop. Gentler or quieter landscapes leave me restless. I know friends who feel more at home working in places of violent conflict rather than relaxing in a rural retreat. It's in the former that they feel most alive, most fully who they are. I can identify with that.

In his memoir *Leaving Alexandria* Richard Holloway talks about life in the Rectory when he was Rector of Old St Paul's in Edinburgh. Not only was there the usual stream of troubled souls and wayfarers coming and going, and sometimes staying, but his family were also trying to live as community with others sharing in the work of the parish. In the stress of all this, Holloway recalls, 'I was becoming increasingly aware that, far from being a sociable creature who liked a lot of people around him, I preferred solitude to society, a good book in my study to a noisy crowd in the kitchen.'[1] Amen to that! By nature I am energized by interaction with the world – I am extrovert in that sense – but increasingly over the years I've needed the balance of being on my own, not relating to anyone, and no one being able to get to me. I no longer need to be at the centre of community life. I'm much more at home 'dancing on the edge' or engaging with communities beyond those with which I'm familiar.

Questions

1 What are the differences between the communities that have been part of your life?
2 What has been your position in these communities in terms of your commitment to them? Are you proactive in the life of a community or do you take a back seat?
3 What does your involvement in these communities tell you about your attitude to community life?

6

I am because we are

————◆◆◆————

Two chapters into the subject and I have not defined what I mean by the word 'community'. The omission is intentional. For the most part we all belong to one or more communities without ever giving much conscious thought to the fact. It's just how things are. I hope the questions I've asked at the end of the previous two chapters, and the whistle-stop tour I've made of some of the communities I've belonged to, have enabled you to reflect a little on your own experience.

A basic definition of community might be a group of people living in the same place or sharing a common vision, purpose, characteristic or interest. Communities take different forms and how we connect with them depends upon the degree to which we feel we do or don't belong to them, and how we develop and change through our lives.

I was born and brought up in the Anglican Church. It has been central to my life. I have always been proactive in its life. I campaigned for the ordination of women to the priesthood in England and was among the first to become a priest in 1994. My professional and personal experience has been shaped significantly by my membership of the Church of England. Recently I became a Quaker. The decision, although right, was a difficult one. I was clear that my understanding, experience and what I held most dear made it impossible for me to remain where I was, but the grief of moving on was also great because it wasn't just that I was part of the community of Anglicans, Anglicanism was part of me, part of my identity. Me as an individual, and me as a member of a community were not two separate things. The extent to which individual identity merges with a communal identity depends upon the extent to which we embrace the latter as our own.

Belonging whether you like it or not

We don't always get to choose the communities we are part of. Family is an obvious example of that. As part of these families we are also part of their wider networks and community contexts in terms of where we live, the school communities we join and the social groups our key carers access. These communities may nurture or undermine our potential. They may feed our curiosity or fuel our contempt for ourselves and others. They may foster a positive sense of identity in us, or leave us feeling useless and worthless. They set patterns of thought and behaviour in us at a point when we are not conscious of the foundations being laid in our hearts and minds. They will shape, for good and ill, how we relate to other individuals and communities throughout our lives. Unless we become conscious of their impact upon us we won't have the opportunity to embrace or reject the messages we picked up as children without realizing we were doing so.

When it comes to the communities we are part of by default rather than conscious decision, we may or may not feel we belong, we may or may not feel happy in them, we may or may not want to play a part in shaping or sustaining them. As with any community of people with different temperaments, levels of power and commitment, clashes of personalities and degrees of belonging and wanting to belong, conflicts will arise that are a normal part of imperfect people interacting and trying to find their way in the world. If we value these communities we will want to belong to them and, in our own particular way, sustain them, working with the negatives and celebrating the positives. If we do not value them and they do not value us, at the first opportunity we will leave.

Choosing to belong out of necessity

Some communities we belong to because they provide us with something we need, although we may not feel entirely at home within them. That is true of some workplace communities. We become part of them because we need to earn a living. We may not share the vision or enthusiasm others have for the work community. We may not prioritize it over other communities to which we belong. We may see this community much more in terms of what we can get from it, as opposed to what we can give to it.

In the workplace we don't necessarily get to choose our colleagues. We may not share the same values. We may have little emotional investment or practical influence in what happens within these communities and this will impact upon our sense of belonging and commitment to the group. Differing levels of commitment to, and expectations of, the work communities we join out of need rather than desire can be a source of conflict.

Choosing to belong because you want to

This belonging may be to a community, like a family, that you didn't choose, but love being part of, and so you remain within it in a variety of different ways that change over time as your life develops. Chosen communities may also be those groups of people you join because you've come to share their beliefs or vision (e.g. a faith community or political party) or have a common interest (e.g. sports clubs or gatherings based on hobbies) or are at a similar life stage (e.g. mother and baby groups, school PTAs, lunch clubs). The fact that we have chosen to be part of these communities means we have an emotional investment in them and a desire to make them flourish. They may reflect key elements of how we understand ourselves to be, as in the case of a person joining a faith community or political party because of what they've come to believe about themselves and others. This emotional investment may lead to greater conflict if the values that are key to our sense of belonging to this group are threatened by outside challenges or by insiders wanting to develop the community in ways counter to our own beliefs. In the case of communities like faith communities or political parties or protest groups, the identity of the community is defined as much by how it differs from other communities as it does on what the members share in common. To be 'not like' another community may also create competition for power and influence, increasing the potential for conflict that may or may not be creative.

The value of community

In general we think of community as being a good thing, but it seems to me, like any other human endeavours, community life has strengths and weaknesses. Much depends upon its internal ethics and the way it understands itself in relation to other communities, particularly those that differ significantly from its own identity.

In recent years, as the world has become 'smaller' in terms of our access to it and we have found ourselves living in the same space as people of other cultures and creeds rather than considering them from a 'safe distance', you can see two major movements at work in response. The first movement is in the direction of reasserting the value of communities with less diversity of creed, culture and identity. In a more controversial expression this might include communities like the English Defence League, but it might also include conservative groups celebrating the more monochrome, less frenetic England either pre-Second World War or in present-day rural idylls that keep historic traditions alive and haven't yet come into the twentieth century!

The second movement welcomes cultural and creedal diversity as a cause for celebration. Those who are part of this community uphold the Golden Rule. This exists in all the major philosophical and religious traditions of the world in a form similar to 'Do unto others as you would have them do unto you'. There is much to commend that rule, but it is also problematic, because it can simply be another way of wanting others to live as you do in a way that lacks any real understanding of who they are. Let me give you an example to explain why.

A nurse I know is very hands-on when people she cares about are ill. She'll sweep in to sick friends with a casserole she made earlier for them, and a kind and generous heart that overflows with good advice and enough energy to tidy up the home she's visiting. She does this because it's the kind of response she appreciates when she's ill. On the other hand, when I am unwell I behave rather like a sick, injured or dying animal. I slip away, curl up, remain very still and prefer to be left on my own. I don't want a fuss made of the fact I'm below par, and I'd rather deal with it in my own way and at my own pace. If my nurse friend came by 'doing as she would be done by', it would not be what I needed at all!

For diverse communities to live harmoniously together we need to go deeper into the 'love your neighbour as yourself' ethos, which is about much more than doing as you would be done by. My sense is that at heart we want to be loved for who we are, not for what others assume we are or expect us to be. This means that when others look at us, or we look at others, we need to get beyond simply recognizing in, or imposing upon, one another reflections of ourselves. We need to learn to see 'face to face', recognizing the reality of the other and being able to discern what they truly need and want, without superimposing our own needs and wants upon them.

I believe this is one of the toughest challenges we face today. How many of the violent conflicts in our world are the result of communities not seeing who the 'other' really is, or respecting their right to be or to live in non-destructive ways different from their own? This same dynamic exists at every level of human community, from family circles to international conflagrations. It's rooted in the arrogant belief that we know best, when in reality it is the result of ignorance, lack of empathy (fellow feeling), fear and hatred. So much damage is done in human communities not by people who are bad but by people who believe they are good and/or right.

Truly understanding ourselves and understanding others demands huge patience, insight, listening and observing skills, selflessness and a whole range of other qualities that I for one am still trying to develop. As a work in progress I am sometimes blind, deaf and inarticulate when it

comes to the needs of others. Paralysed by my own fears and inadequacies I am not able or willing to walk the extra mile to understand
where you stand. Such is the human condition, which is why in my
own scriptural tradition we have stories of Jesus opening the eyes of the
blind, unstopping the ears of the deaf, enabling the dumb to speak and
helping the lame and paralysed to walk. The power of these stories,
in my view, doesn't lie in them being actual physical events in one time
and place, but in making visible the action of love, fleshed out in human
form in all times and places, transforming our blind, deaf, inarticulate,
lame and paralysed perceptions. These changes don't happen all at once.
Nor can they happen in isolation of others, because we can be very
good at deceiving ourselves. It's worth noting that those who can help
us to see our own limitations are often members of communities to
which we don't belong. That's because they can see the questions to ask
that people like us can't because we share the same assumptions.

Perhaps, most of all, developing understanding requires the ability
to hold steady in the face of opposition, heightened emotion and the
taking of sides by everyone around you. This in turn is dependent upon
us being secure enough in our own identity to step into a position of
potentially solitary vulnerability in order to transform a situation and
to maintain an ethical position.

St John tells the story of a group of men bringing an adulterous
woman to Jesus and demanding to know what he thinks should happen
to her, given that the law says she must be stoned to death. I'll be
exploring this story in more depth in a later chapter. What is important
to note here is that Jesus does not leap into taking sides. He does not
get caught up in the emotion around him but diffuses it. He does not
seek to overpower the men by dominating them. Indeed, in physical
terms, he takes the posture of one who is of lesser stature and power,
literally crouching down to draw in the sand. When he speaks, his words,
'Let him who is without sin cast the first stone', get to the heart of the
issue without humiliating his listeners. He takes them seriously, and
sees who they really are, so he is able to speak in a way they can hear,
understand and respond to appropriately. His depth of awareness of the
people before him means he is able to deal justly with the problem and
not escalate it further.

Giving the 2013 Elson Ethics lecture for St George's House, Windsor
Castle, Professor Mervyn Frost raised the question of why groups like
al-Qaeda, which are numerically small and militarily limited in relation
to 'Goliaths' like the United States, have impacted so much upon these
superpowers. While the destroying of the Twin Towers on September
11th was a terrible tragedy, it did not threaten the military might of the
US, nor was the loss of life comparable to the loss of Iraqi and Afghan

lives in the violence resulting from British and American military action in those places. Frost talked about 'ethical fouls' and pointed out how the actions of al-Qaeda have been successful because their own ethical fouls have prompted superpowers like America to respond with ethical fouls, thereby losing the moral high ground they believe they have. It's a thought-provoking theory.

Think too of the use of chemical weapons in the civil war in Syria on 21 August 2013. It appeared to produce a knee-jerk reaction from David Cameron and Barak Obama, with the threat of a military strike in Syria by the UK and the USA looking to be an imminent response intended to deter the use of further chemical weapons, and all this before the UN chemical weapons investigators had finished their work in Syria, let alone analysed the material they had collected and submitted their report. It seemed, once more, that an ethical foul was about to prompt another ethical foul by Western powers. Thankfully, by the time Cameron had recalled Parliament, there had been time for members to 'draw in the sand' and to decide against a plan of unethical violent action without having exhausted all the political means of resolving this complex, heart-breaking example of communal violent conflict and community breakdown. The decision did not guarantee an appropriate ethical resolution and some might argue that the lack of intervention has itself proved to be unethical in the light of the ongoing suffering of the Syrian people, but I was relieved we didn't follow through with knee-jerk responses we knew from past experience might be equally destructive or worse.

The ability to hold steady in the face of communal tension and conflict, secure in our own identity, attentive to the identity and needs of others, and committed to responding ethically, is as crucial now to the well-being of human community as ever it was, and we struggle to embody such a way of being as much as we ever did, individually and communally.

What does all this mean?

It means that we need to mind the gap between the lip-service we pay to the idea of community and the reality most of us live. We may love the idea of hospitable, inclusive community, secure in its own identity and open to the experience of others, but how many of us are actually prepared to put in the effort required in order to create such communities?

Responsibilities as well as rights

The relationship between rights and responsibilities is a critical one when it comes to community life. I am conscious of my desire for the benefits of being part of a community, while struggling to bear my share of the responsibility for making it work. Part of the problem is that I belong to many different communities and I can't give 100 per cent to all of them. I simply can't stretch myself that thinly.

Most communities tend to rely on a minority to keep them going, a core group who manage the day-to-day life of the community. Other members are less active or silent, or they come and go, or they grumble about what's not right in the community but do nothing to help make things better!

Holding diversity?

It is one thing to value diversity in a community, but the well-being of that community depends upon it having sufficient common ground among its members in order to be secure in its identity. As a community changes and develops, new ideas, practices and people will become part of it, but the health of the community may also depend upon it some-times being able to say when a difference in perception is a difference too far from the *raison d'être* of that community.

For example, one of the questions with which the Church of England is wrestling is whether or not it truly wishes to be a broad Church in which people with sometimes diametrically opposed views and beliefs can still see each other as family. If it does, what is it that unites us as community? If it doesn't, wouldn't it be better to be honest, because the ability to create a community celebrating and sometimes struggling with diversity is undermined when what people really want is for those who don't share their vision to leave the fold?

I find the example of the Quakers deeply moving, with Christian Quakers, Buddhist Quakers, even atheist Quakers feeling at home together, sharing a common commitment to silence and to social justice, and valuing a space in which people are not told what to believe but given the space and opportunity to work out their own understanding, sup-ported and encouraged by those around them who do not claim to have the whole truth and nothing but the truth.

I suspect that most of us struggle with getting the balance right between enjoying the benefits of community life and bearing the cost of it. Some of us expend ourselves for the sake of the community to such an extent that our family suffers – clergy have something of a propensity for this state of affairs. Their sense of responsibility is over-sized, perhaps even tinged with something of a Messiah complex. They forget that cemeteries are full of people who thought themselves indispensable. Others of us put little into the community while expecting it constantly to meet our needs. Most of us probably fall between these two extremes. Few of us, I suspect, find it easy to sacrifice our own needs for the greater good of the group.

Sacrifice is an uncomfortable, even 'dirty', word, particularly in a society where many people expect to be able to have what they want regardless of the consequences for others, for the wider world or, in the long term, for themselves. Short-term satisfaction takes priority. Perhaps we find it easier to bury our heads in the sand. Someone else can deal with it – back to the notion of responsibility. If we head into environmental catastrophe or global conflict, it won't be because no one warned us we were heading in that direction, or that nobody was trying to do anything to prevent such disasters. It will be because too few of us played our part in turning around the human juggernaut heading for ultimate annihilation. We need to reclaim not only a sense of personal responsibility supported by corporate action, but also the recognition that if our children and grandchildren are going to have a positive future, we need to make significant sacrifices in the present. This will not come easily, since it is clear that whatever our aspirations regarding community living, we frequently fail to live them out. In part this is because we struggle to hold the tension between 'I' and 'We', between my needs and the needs of other people. So let's turn in Chapter 7 to the struggle to be selfless when being selfish is so much easier.

Questions

1 What is your level of commitment to the communities to which you belong?
2 Do you feel you have the right balance between your rights and responsibilities in those communities?
3 How could you be more effective in the context of community?

Part 3

GREED

7

What's yours is mine!

Sometimes when the doorbell rings my heart sinks. I know it will be one particular rough sleeper who periodically calls round asking for money. As a clergy family we are used to wayfarers on the doorstep. Usually we make up food parcels and occasionally give cash. We meet some extraordinary rough sleepers but there is one caller I cannot abide.

'Greetings, Sister!' he will say with exaggerated bonhomie as I open the door. I can feel my hackles rising. He has come with one purpose only: to get money. Once he receives it, he will leave, returning only when he needs the next handout. His cheeriness of salutation is not because he is pleased to see us. He does not care how we are or what is going on in our lives. All he wants is our money. If we question the story he tells us in order to elicit our sympathy and support, he comes up with another, then another. Who can blame him? If my experience had been his, who is to say I wouldn't behave in exactly the same way in order to survive? There but for the grace of God . . . And yet he infuriates me.

Once he came when my husband Chris had just arrived home after major surgery. I was feeling utterly exhausted.

'My husband is ill,' I said, 'I can't deal with your demands as well.'

He left immediately. I felt bad, and then I felt angry for feeling bad.

Other homeless men who call at our door do not trigger the same response in me. Some of them we have come to know over time. One or two come in for a hot meal or a shower. They don't want us to do more. They have dignity and we try to do what we can without undermining that. But this man enrages me.

The loss of generosity

My reaction is far removed from how my 20-year-old self responded to the needs of others. At a recent reunion, friends from my days as a student nurse at St Thomas's Hospital reminded me of an incident I had forgotten. Returning to the nurses' home after seeing a film in Leicester Square, they recalled me leaping out of a taxi into the freezing night and running off in pursuit of a homeless and inadequately dressed 'bag lady' to give her my duffle coat. I feel both embarrassed by and wistful about this younger self who responded not because it was expected of her, nor because it was necessarily the 'right thing' to do, but because that's what she felt moved to do in the moment. Her compassion was heartfelt and spontaneous.

What happened to her?

She remains a part of my essential self. At one level she has developed some maturity. Disappearing off into the night and returning late with total disregard for the anxiety my actions provoked in my friends was thoughtless. Understanding that, at times, saying 'no' to someone in need because the needs of others rightly take priority is a step forward. But over the years the spontaneous generosity of my younger self has been almost sucked dry by seemingly endless demands. I have been complicit in her shrivelling, often working without pay on projects I thought made a difference to people in difficulty, because making a difference not making a mint was my priority. In my early adult life I believed it was what God wanted of me and that if I did the 'right thing' God would take care of me. In the back of my mind I thought some of the projects might lead to further work: self-interest and altruism in step together. Sometimes that happened, but payment was fitful. Churches, particularly, expected me to work for free or for a book token, neither of which helps to pay bills. Good will is often greatly abused in communities where self-sacrifice for the sake of others is held in high regard. While I could ask for appropriate payment for other people, I found it hard to do for myself, so we struggled to meet household expenses and wondered how we would manage in what was then far-off retirement.

There is nothing quite so effective in quelling a generous and self-giving nature than other people *expecting* you to be generous and self-giving. It takes away the spontaneity and leaves the bitter taste of feeling used and inappropriately valued. When the homeless man I find difficult turns up on my doorstep with his particular way of demanding help regardless of what may be going on for me, my animosity is stirred. Is there nowhere I can go, including my own home, without someone wanting something from me, even when I feel down to my last reserve? At heart I know my antagonism towards my inadequate visitor is a rage against personal inadequacy of which he reminds me. When I open the door and feel my hackles rise at the sight and sound of him, it is not primarily him that I am reacting against but the reflection of me in him that I recognize at some level of my being.

The three goblets

Some years ago, when I first became aware of this inner conflict, a friend asked me to picture three goblets into which wine continually drips. The first, he said, has holes in the cup so the wine leaks out even as it drips in, and the goblet never fills. The second is free of holes but the sides extend upwards so that although the wine level rises it too is never full. The third has neither holes nor extending sides. When it becomes full it naturally overflows.

'Which of these do you identify with?' asked my friend.

'I want to be the third,' I said, 'but the truth is I alternate between the first two.'

Putting aside those times in life when things are tough and demanding for reasons beyond our control, I suspect that being like the goblet with holes, always giving out and never becoming full to overflowing, is generally to do with inadequate levels of self-awareness, self-esteem and self-confidence. The situation with the second goblet, on the other hand, is more often due to a lack of awareness about or care for others, or an ignorantly inflated sense of self or a traumatized heart that hangs on to the trickle of positive input in a partial state of paralysis, fearing every drip might be the last.

At those times when I've felt utterly drained and have nothing left to give, like a car that's run out of petrol and not been refilled, I switch into the mindset of the second goblet, holding to myself any refreshment that comes my way, reluctant to share it with others. After all, I tell myself, I have so much in the way of lost resources to replenish, and who knows when anything else life-giving will come my way, or the next disaster explode into my experience. Generosity is the last thing on my mind, and I'll do all I can to block from consciousness the needs of others, excluding perhaps those closest to me. ME (and MINE) dominate my priorities.

Few people have lives of permanent equilibrium where they are consistently full to overflowing. Sometimes even the naturally overflowingly generous person runs a bit low and needs to take time out to replenish their resources. I meet many people embodying either the first or the second goblet, or lurching between the two. The third remains more elusive, and those who give expression to it in their encounters with others are a gift of rare delight, as is the experience of being the third goblet.

Attempting to be the third goblet

The reality of the three goblets is poignantly personified in Rembrandt's *Return of the Prodigal Son* (reproduced overleaf).

Rembrandt, *Return of the Prodigal Son*

It captures the climax of the well-known parable about the son who takes his inheritance without thought to anyone else (the second goblet), leaves home and squanders what he has been given. In a state of destitution he determines to return to his father with rehearsed words of apology he hopes will be enough to ensure his acceptance back into the family fold and the comfortable life he once had. As things turn out, his manipulative apology is pre-empted by his father's response when, from a distance, he sees him returning. Ignoring social conventions concerning a man of high status, the father rushes out to greet his wayward son, his arms wide open and no apparent reproach on his lips (the third goblet).

Overwhelmed by this experience of unconditional love, the son's contrived words of repentance and shallow role-play of penitence fall from him. Suddenly all the tension, grief and longing leave him and he sinks to his knees as though his whole body is letting go. His shoe falls off. Held in his father's embrace he loses his psychological footing and experiences a genuine and deep change of heart. Paradoxically as he falls apart, his self is restored.

In the shadows stands his brother. He has always done the right thing, working tirelessly for his father, regardless of what he might want for himself (the first goblet). In the light of his father's unconditional love for his wayward brother he is deeply resentful, sucked dry of generosity.

Recognizing the older brother in our own psyche

When we get things wrong and let others down the experience of another person's unconditional acceptance and embrace is indeed the catalyst for deepening our understanding and making positive changes in our lives, but such empathetic encounters are not common currency. In the face of personal failing many of us are met with the reaction of the older brother lurking in the shadows, who wants us to suffer for our sins. 'His' harshness of response makes dealing with the issues much harder because it prompts us to pull up the drawbridge and take cover behind personal defences as a means of protecting ourselves against the slings and arrows of his self-righteous judgement and desire for vengeance. And yet . . . In truth, when I have been in that older brother's position, offended by the betrayal and abuse of others, I too have felt as he does. Part of my pilgrimage in more recent years is about trying to bring my reactions when confronted by the failings of others more into line with the reactions I need from others when I am the one who has failed.

Selfish acquisition vs authentic self-giving

Bearing in mind my friend's images of the three goblets (particularly the potential unconscious greediness of the first cup and the deliberate greed of the second cup), and the overflowing generosity of the father captured in Rembrandt's *The Return of the Prodigal*, I want to reflect on the tightrope we walk between selfish acquisition and authentic self-giving.

An extreme example of the former is the global financial crisis of 2007/08. It threatened the total collapse of large financial institutions. Banks were bailed out by national governments. Stock markets plummeted. Businesses failed. In some places housing markets went awry. Global recession ensued. In the UK, as in many other countries, there was a major public backlash against 'fat-cat bankers' who had lined their own pockets at the expense of those who had little in the way of pockets, let alone the cash with which to line them. The injustice was evident, the anger understandable. Change in economic policy and practice was, and remains, essential.

One of the ingredients in this melting pot of economic crisis and human pain has been a response reminiscent of vintage Hollywood classics in which the 'goodies', who are all good, confront the 'baddies', who are all bad. Many people (the goodies) living with the consequences of the bankers' (the baddies) choices still feel as though the baddies, albeit chastened, remain on top, creaming off their bonuses while the brunt of cutbacks, job losses and debt is borne by the most vulnerable people in our society. Those feelings are justified, but they are also too simplistic.

They create the kind of 'us' and 'them' mentality that constantly prevents us from dealing well with the problems life throws up.

Scapegoating others

Our capacity to shift the blame for what happens to us on to others and to the world in which we live is boundless and seemingly innate. Climbing into the car when she was about three years old, my daughter Freya bashed her head on the door frame. Once the tears were over her first words were, 'Mummy, it's all your fault: you weren't looking where I was going.'

Her words made me laugh but the same trait in adult behaviour can be crucifying. Unless we take responsibility for what is our responsibility, necessary change cannot happen.

Some ancient biblical communities dealt with their individual and group wrongdoing by annually taking time to own up to their iniquities. Once they'd done that they placed their combined screw-ups symbolically on to a goat – the scapegoat – which was then driven into the wilderness. The ritual left the people feeling the burden of their foul-ups had been taken away and they could start afresh.

In the present day we use the term 'scapegoat' to suggest the opposite. If I use you as a scapegoat it has nothing to do with me owning up to blowing things once again. I blame you for what I can't be honest about in me. My mistakes, or this mess I'm in, are your fault not mine. In his book *Falling Upward*,[1] Franciscan priest Richard Rohr writes of the crucifixion of Jesus: 'The cross solved our problem by first revealing our real problem – our universal pattern of scapegoating and sacrificing others. The cross exposes forever the "scene of our crime."' Scapegoating others for our own destructive behaviour is one of the greatest delusions of all time. The attraction of it is that it removes from us any personal responsibility to address what has gone pear-shaped. *It's your problem not mine!*

The elusiveness of truth

Even in circumstances where guilt appears clear-cut, the truth may be rather more complicated. Can there be any doubt the violence in Northern Ireland was solely down to the actions of Loyalist and Republican paramilitary groups? I didn't think so, until my work required me to learn about and work in that context. The people I met drew my attention to the fact, for example, that churches speaking out against the violence also perpetuated beliefs that fuelled division between Catholics and Protestants. Members sent their children to schools that only accepted children of their denomination, so it was much harder for each to see the human face of the other. Many who longed for peace nevertheless voted for politicians whose policies discriminated against those they did not want to see in power. How many, as in any other place, accepted the status quo until the results of it began to impact negatively on them personally?

A friend of mine was crossing Westminster Bridge when a man climbed on to the wall with the intention of jumping off and drowning himself. My friend and her partner grabbed him and tried to pull him back, calling to some other passers-by to get the police they'd noticed at the end of the bridge. 'Oh no,' came the reply. 'We're only watching.' They did not want to get involved, and yet by choosing to do nothing they were involved. It is a fallacy to think that when we do nothing we are taking a neutral position. When someone does something wrong they do not want others to take action. On the other hand, the victim of their wrongful behaviour wants others to act. To do nothing is therefore to collude with the perpetrator. It is to allow them to continue unchallenged.

That is what happened in relation to the global financial crisis. While the financial systems worked in our favour, how many of us turned a blind eye to the way in which they helped to keep the majority of the world's peoples in poverty and developed business practices that were lucrative in the short term but unsustainable and detrimental to long-term economic stability? How many of us claimed ignorance at what was going on, as if ignorance when we have the opportunity to learn more is a viable excuse? When it suits our personal interests, all of us have the capacity to shut out uncomfortable truths. This is made much easier if we stick with people who see life as we do. They won't ask us difficult questions or challenge our blind spots.

'Us' and 'Them'?

Alongside this personally challenging awareness is the equally uncomfortable realization that 'they' often share more in common with 'us' than we might like to acknowledge, even when stepping into their space feels like entering a completely different world. It has been suggested that the active phase of the global financial crisis of 2007/08 can be dated from 7 August when one of the world's largest global banking groups, BNP Paribas, terminated withdrawals from three hedge funds citing 'a complete evaporation of liquidity'. In 2011 and 2012 I gave lectures on human perception and diversity in the London Headquarters of BNP Paribas. The bankers attending my lectures were intelligent, dynamic women and men; people with whom I could talk easily, people like those I meet in many other areas of life, people, in many respects, like me. I did not recognize in them the fat-cat caricatures that have littered media representations of them. They were flawed human beings like the rest of us. The one key difference was that they had the power and position that enabled the potential for greed we share in common to be given legitimacy, and to impact detrimentally not just on individuals but on global populations.

I know that the capacity to take what I can get and give nothing or little in return comes from a crippled part of my make-up. It is a symptom of a self that has suffered in some way and in response to that suffering has shut down to the suffering of others, becoming selfish rather than selfless. Greed and selfish action are symptomatic of a damaged self. In my experience the abuse of power is often rooted in an earlier experience of being abused when in the position of being powerless. 'Never again', I say, 'am I going to be vulnerable in that way.'

I may not have the power to make decisions that have a national or global impact, but I'm only too aware of sometimes behaving in ways I know hurt others in order to stop them hurting me. The more independent and impregnable a life I can create for myself, the better. To live a defensive, protected life may hold harm of a particular kind at bay, but it also confines our humanity and in the long term we are the losers. In the end I would rather take the hurt that comes with living a generous and compassionate life than the suffering that results from a self-defensive, desiccated existence.

To recognize that greed and the abuse of power may be rooted in painful past experiences of being powerless is not to justify such things, but it should impact upon the way we deal with or try to prevent them. In his first Easter sermon as Archbishop of Canterbury, Justin Welby said:

> Put not your trust in new leaders, better systems, new organizations or regulatory reorganization. They may well be good and necessary, but will to some degree fail. Human sin means pinning hopes on individuals is always a mistake, and assuming that any organization is able to have such good systems that human failure will be eliminated is naive.

This being the case we need to be realistic about human nature, and develop individually and corporately an approach to human institutions that is both critical and compassionate. Critical because we know just how fallible we all are, and compassionate for exactly the same reason!

Questions

1 With which of the three goblets do you most identify?
2 How do the prodigal son, the unconditionally loving parent and the resentful sibling play out in your own psyche?
3 Who do you scapegoat for your own failings?

8

Our blinded sight

Getting to grips with the capacity for greed we all have is clearly an important thing to do, but there's a problem. What happens when the society in which we live *encourages* human traits that need to be held in check? For example, to defend our country young men and women are trained to kill. It's hardly surprising then, that some veterans returning from the field of battle and suffering from post-traumatic stress disorder find it hard to contain this heightened aspect of their experience in peacetime. Ex-combatants have a higher incidence of becoming homeless, ending up in prison, coping with broken relationships or committing suicide than their non-military counterparts. Likewise, certain professions encourage attitudes like greed, which can be deeply destructive. The purpose of most businesses is to make a profit. The bigger the profit, the better it is. 'Doing well' means making money for your company, bank or business. In highly competitive markets ruthlessness may become part of team tactics and ethics may be unceremoniously kicked into touch. Working environments, like the trading floors of banks, cease to be healthy spaces. This is even reflected in their physical layout. In her book *Quiet*, Susan Cain points out that there is a 'mountain of recent data' that shows open-plan offices

> reduce productivity and impair memory. They're associated with high staff turnover. They make people sick, hostile, unmotivated, and insecure. Open-plan workers are more likely to suffer from high blood pressure ... elevated stress levels and to get the flu. They argue more with their colleagues ... They're often subjected to loud and uncontrollable noise, which raises heart rates; releases cortisol, the body's fight-or-flight 'stress' hormone; and makes people socially distant, quick to anger, aggressive, and slow to help others.[1]

The less immediate and the more elusive the consequences of how you achieve profit, the easier it is to act without awareness of or attention to those consequences. How often does the trader at her computer screen connect with the poverty, destitution and conflict that result from the same business, national and international economic policies from which she profits? It is easy to become caught up in the personal desire for success regardless of the consequences of that for people you cannot see and do not know. Even if a person is aware of the negative consequences of making money in the way they do, it is hard to take a stand against the financial juggernaut of which they may be only one small cog.

Whistle-blowers

If a working culture thrives on greed, competition and winning at all costs, any person within that environment who questions the ethics of what's going on will not be welcome. This is not just true of businesses where the purpose is profit. People who have spoken out about poor care and abuse in the NHS, or staff bullying in schools and media organizations, have sometimes been the butt of reprisals, or subject to disciplinary procedures, or lost their jobs before their truth-telling to power is finally proved accurate and changes are made. For some there is no justice and they are left by the roadside, the casualties of corrupt colleagues and corporations.

That we have the term 'whistle-blower' indicates how unhealthy many of our institutions and organizations have become. Working environments should be places where we are expected to talk constructively about what is or isn't working. We should be able to speak out without fear of being labelled negatively as whistle-blowers when we draw attention to injustice and abuses of power. Inevitably, this may sometimes result in conflict, but conflict is not necessarily a bad thing, as I'll explore later in this book.

If we are not attentive the culture of competitive organizations can bring out the worst in their members and work in favour of people or processes that may become abusive. From a survival point of view, being competitive might be argued to be essential, but the other side of that coin is that it can divide and distance people from one another and be detrimental to human well-being. In the story of the prodigal son we see how sibling rivalry contaminates the relationship between the brothers. *He's getting more than I am, and it's not fair!* What happens to compassionate humanity when aggressive competition is a factor in the human equation?

One casualty may be good team relationships between staff. Team work is important but team members may be in competition for the same jobs and promotion. This makes trust difficult. What happens to our humanity when we consider the value of others only in terms of their benefit or threat to us? The father in the parable of the prodigal son operates by the principle of 'win–win'. He wants things to be good for both his sons. The older brother sees the welcome extended to his prodigal sibling as something of a defeat for himself. For him it's a 'win–lose' situation with himself as the loser. The younger brother doesn't really seem to have considered anyone but himself until he experiences his father's unconditional embrace.

The third goblet in the boardroom?

In competitive environments the danger is that the condition of the first and second goblets I mentioned earlier dominates at the expense of the third. Some draw more and more of the profits to themselves, taking beyond what is needful and right, while others feel drained by the system and either struggle on or fall by the wayside. Wouldn't it make more sense to work in a way that enables every person to become appropriately full and naturally overflow, rather than maintain the haves and the have-nots? Yet, human resource directors I speak with in international businesses often feel they are fighting a losing battle in trying to get their company high-flyers to recognize the importance to long-term success of enabling staff at every level to flourish. By definition the system has worked for the high-flyers, so they may have little impetus to change it. Never mind the ones who have fallen by the wayside! They are easily replaceable. *There was probably something wrong with them anyway,* those who succeed in the system may say. *If they can't stand the heat . . . !*

Me too!

Over the years of listening to people from all walks of life and seeing how I respond for good or ill in different situations, I've come to the conclusion that there is no human institution where the abuse of power and dehumanizing pressures and processes do not exist. None of us is free of the potential to lack integrity in thought, word and action. Individually, whatever our background and circumstances, there will have been times when we have received or taken something at the expense of someone else. How many of us buy cheap clothing knowing the working conditions of those making the garments fall below acceptable standards and may even be regarded as slave labour? How many of us buy cheap food that comes at a cost to animal welfare or environmental sustainability? How many of us use resources the production of which contributes to climate change and natural catastrophe, usually in other parts of the world with which we have little connection? How many of us have, at some time or other, ignored the possible consequences of our actions upon others in order to get something we want or need?

How many of us find ways of justifying personal actions that in others we would find 'unjustifiable'?

The blindness of the older brother?

In Rembrandt's painting, this older brother simmers in the shadows, oblivious to the transformation his father's loving response has upon the son kneeling dishevelled at the old man's feet. The embrace between them sickens him. He wants that good-for-nothing to be publicly hauled over the coals for all the mistakes he's made, mistakes of which he, the elder brother, thinks himself innocent.

It may well be that the mistakes of the two brothers are not the same, but that is a very different thing from the self-righteousness of the older brother who thinks himself blameless. His lack of self-awareness leads to a vindictiveness that does him little credit.

The dynamics at work in the reaction of this resentful brother were very visible in the responses of the news media and the general public to the global financial crisis. How many of us took the moral high ground as though we were completely selfless innocents who always did the right and dutiful thing, and had never benefited from the economic systems we condemned when they all went wrong? Did the vilification of 'fat-cat bankers' do anything more than satisfy a public need to see someone pay heavily for unethical economic systems that have flourished because few of us bothered to question their existence? Major public protests came far too late, when the damage was already done.

Like many of the parables of Jesus, the story of the prodigal son, through the response of the father, emphasizes mercy and grace. Perhaps that's because Jesus lived in a time when there was a great deal of punishment and public humiliation running hand in hand with self-righteous religious judgement. It is a lethal combination and one that exists as much today as it did in the time of Jesus. The selfish, self-destructive irresponsibility and greed of the prodigal son and the self-righteous, ignorant, condemnation of the older brother are traits common to all human beings in all times and places.

Group induced self-deception

There is another dynamic at work in relation to negative human traits which we have touched on but not explored in depth – peer pressure. Neuroscientist Gregory S. Berns and his team used MRI scanning to determine which parts of the brain were activated when 32 volunteers worked as a group and either conformed to group opinion or broke from it.[2] His research showed that group members conformed not because they decided consciously to go along with what they knew to be the wrong answer or action, but because their perceptions were changed by the group. It seems it is not only difficult to speak out when you are a minority voice, but also that your correct perceptions can be changed by the influence of the group. I am aware of this dynamic in everyday family life and at work. Time and again at the school where I was chaplain students got into trouble doing things they knew to be wrong but that, when with their friends, suddenly seemed acceptable.

I can see this behaviour writ large in the international affairs of adults, particularly in acts of human atrocity. In her 1963 work *Eichmann in Jerusalem: A Report on the Banality of Evil*,[3] Hannah Arendt concluded from her research that the great evils in history generally, and in the Holocaust specifically, were not perpetrated by sociopaths or fanatics but by ordinary people who had come to accept the perspective put forward by the State and to see their actions as normal. From a distance of both time and space it is hard to understand how ordinary people could accept as normal such terrible inhumanity as genocide, but even in our own lives we can see the power of peer pressure and herd mentality. Whether we play an active part in perpetuating unhealthy systems or are complicit in their persistence through apathy, the fear of speaking out or the 'I'm all right, Jack' mentality, none of us can claim to be innocent.

Going forward

If the global financial crisis illustrates anything at all it is how hard we find it to hold in sight the humanity others share with us. If we understand that common bond, in the words of Rowan Williams, 'we can't say that what is unwelcome or evil for us is tolerable for others'.[4] While I must sometimes face unwelcome truths, I do not want to experience unnecessary pain and anguish caused by the inhumanity of others. This being the case how can I accept any system or institution that imposes pain and anguish on other people through its processes? Thinking back to the three goblets, it is wholly unacceptable to drain another of what little they do have in their lives, or to hold to ourselves as much as we can, leaving others to go without. The aim is to make sure each has enough to be full and overflow naturally. Our common humanity rules out the application of the 'one rule for "us" and another rule for "them"' behaviour we get caught up in all too easily.

In an assembly, I was showing Year 7 and 8 students pictures of grotesque pollution in other parts of the world. They gasped in horror at some of the images. 'It shouldn't be allowed,' they said. 'The people who made this mess should clear it up,' they said. 'Why don't those people take care of their environment,' they said. 'Are they stupid?' And then I brought up on the screen some images from closer to home, in fact of our own school at the end of break-time. There were photos of sweet papers, crisp packets and drinks cartons littering the corridors, and of waste bins with rubbish scattered beneath them. I said I thought they were absolutely right to be disgusted by the pollution in the pictures they had seen, and to expect those responsible to clear it up or, more importantly, not to make it in the first place, but, I wondered, why do you expect of others what you are not doing yourselves?

The obvious answer to that question is that it is much easier to see and criticize the errors of others than to acknowledge and address personal failings: to criticize the 'speck' in the eye of another rather than deal with the 'log' in my own (Luke 6.41–42). As the kids at school might think, if none of my friends are bothering to clear up their rubbish, why should I clear up mine? It's not even discussed. It is taken as the norm. Peer pressure doesn't need words to 'work'.

A common knee-jerk response when I asked a student to pick up a piece of litter was, 'But I didn't drop it, Ruth.' Their expectation was that someone else would clear up the mess. It wasn't their responsibility. They were happy to take whatever school offered, but had little commitment to building community life in school and beyond. If things were not working properly it was everybody else's responsibility but their own. During my time in school I became aware of what seemed to be a growing sense of entitlement among some students who came with a high expectation of what they should be getting, but had little expectation of what they might give. This is learnt behaviour and reflects the example of key adults in their lives. Would that each of us was as greedy to give of ourselves as we may be greedy to take for ourselves.

If we choose to live in a way that doesn't cause others the kind of suffering we wouldn't accept for ourselves then we must always question the purpose of human systems and institutions. If they are to enhance human life and to enable us to maintain the world in which we live for the well-being not only of ourselves but for future generations we cannot accept financial set-ups that keep the majority of the world's people in poverty, unable to tackle treatable illnesses, eradicate famine, deal with environmental disasters, avoid destructive conflict and generally stand with dignity in the world as we seek to do.

Affirming life

In the Christian story, when the women come to the tomb of Jesus on Easter morning two unearthly characters confront them with the question, 'Why do you seek the living among the dead?' It is a question we would do well to ask ourselves regularly today. When we focus on the inanimate things of life, like money and possessions, instead of living fleshed-out human relations and the flora and fauna of our fabulous world, we put ourselves or others in a grave situation that will ultimately be the death of us, or of our children's children. To be self-centred is to entomb ourselves.

Focusing on life beyond our own small world more often than not means being prepared to hold different needs in tension, just as the father of the prodigal son seeks to hold in tension the differing experiences and needs of his two sons. Where does love offer the freedom for exploration and where does it speak in a firmer voice? Let me give an example from my school experience to help to illustrate the tension that comes with being focused on the living rather than the dead.

One of the balances that teaching and support staff worked hard to get right, and were frequently reassessing, concerned what rules were essential to the school working well and what flexibility must be safeguarded so that we didn't turn out robots but real people, capable of thinking for themselves, being creative and ready to engage with wider life and take flight. New students arrived who, as a result of inadequate parenting, had no sense at all of boundaries. They kicked off all over the place like diminutive Jekyll and Hyde characters, refusing to do anything that didn't suit them. They were profoundly unhappy. Some were crying out for clear-cut rules with consequences for those who broke them. They fought against it, but they needed the containment they'd never properly had. The chaos of their circumstances overwhelmed them, and until they began to adhere to basic rules they were cut off from their capacity for creativity. I have always been an advocate for unconditional love, although I have rarely succeeded in living it with my own children, but unconditional love should not be confused with the notion that anything goes.

The prodigal son, loved unconditionally by his father, but feeling confined by his way of life, removes himself from the sphere of his father's love once he has the freedom provided by his inheritance. He goes off, lives riotously, discovers and tests his own limits and learns some very hard lessons. He discovers that total freedom without responsibility is not freedom. He hits rock bottom, faces his failure and realizes he needs some containment if he is to be truly free. He returns home where the unconditional love of his father awaits him. His brother, in contrast, plays by the rules. He does the 'right' thing. He takes no risks. He expects reward. He is free to come and go like his brother, yet he stays safe and sulks when his wayward sibling returns to celebration not censure. His attitude imprisons the life in him. The prodigal son kneels dishevelled at his father's feet, and yet it seems to me that he is a better person by far than his obedient brother, standing sourly in the suffocating shadow of his personal self-righteous self-pity.

The parable seems to affirm not only the father's love but the prodigal son's risk-taking and return. He engages with life, gets things wrong, fails, falls and, in that falling, rises: yet another example in biblical tradition of a deeply flawed and failing person who somehow becomes the means of divine grace. The ones who receive the greatest censure from Jesus are self-righteous religious people. I accept these things not because the Bible tells me so, but because I have found the same grace among the 'fallen' and the same brittle inhumanity among self-righteous people, believers or atheists, who have never risked failure. The key difference between the two groups is that the former own their flaws and failings and learn to work with them while the latter are blind to the possibility that they may be wrong.

If we expect our businesses, organizations and institutions to be run by flawless people we are on a hiding to nothing. No one is incapable of greed or the abuse of power. If we recognize that these systems will always be the work of flawed human hands, including our own, then we open up the possibility of not only minimizing the human cost of our faults and failings in this context, but of working compassionately with them in such a way that success is not achieved at the expense of others, but for the benefit of all. So let's turn our attention now to our capacity or otherwise for compassion.

Questions

1 Where does your own capacity for greed find expression?
2 When do you, through your actions or lack of action, allow others to suffer in ways you would not tolerate yourself?
3 What can you do to change things for the better?

Part 4

COMPASSION

9

No more Mr Nice Guy

In recent years the news media have covered a seemingly endless stream of stories about poor care, neglect and downright cruelty in the NHS and in care homes for elderly residents or severely disabled adults. It seems incomprehensible that organizations set up with the specific task of caring for the most vulnerable people in our society should lack the one thing essential to their work – compassion.

Compassion is the ability to understand at a heartfelt level the experience of another person. It is a key, but not exclusively, Christian quality. That said, there's plenty of evidence to suggest that Christians have over the centuries lacked compassion as much as the incompetent and cruel nurses and care home workers who have been on the receiving end of so much media attention and public contempt. In fact, if we look at any group within human society, whatever their religious affiliation or lack of it, the picture is very much the same. While publicly applauding compassionate action, many people struggle privately to act compassionately at times. In this chapter I want to explore why, despite our aspirations, living with compassion is so much more difficult than we often care to own. My starting point is a parable that was once familiar to most people in the UK but now seems to be falling into obscurity.

Who is my neighbour?

Recent research carried out by Durham University discovered that 60 per cent of those interviewed did not know the story of the good Samaritan from the Gospel of Luke. Jesus tells the parable when he is exploring with his listeners the commandments to love God and love your neighbour.

'Who is my neighbour?' asks a lawyer in the crowd. Jesus tells how a member of their community, travelling from Jerusalem to Jericho, is mugged and left for dead. Seeing the injured man, a priest and a Levite from his community pass by on the other side. It is a Samaritan, an outsider, who comes to the victim's aid.

Samaritans were regarded with suspicion, if not hatred, by those listening to the story. The parable was profoundly controversial because it redefined 'neighbour' to mean everyone, including those considered to be the enemy. Working in communities living with the legacy of violent conflict I also find myself wondering what it must be like to be in the position of the injured man when we find ourselves being cared for by those whom we think of as an enemy.

Two thousand years later people of faith who are unaware of the enmities that gave this story particular bite in its own time are more likely to find controversial the fact that it was the religious leaders of Jesus' day who, due to the laws regarding ritual purity, did nothing to help the injured man. Even among non-religious people there is a popular expectation that religious people should be good, or at least behave better than anyone else, not least because they go on about human virtues. Some religionists have certainly set themselves up to be seen in that way but it's only part of the picture. There are many more people like me, who are drawn to faith precisely because we know how short of our aspirations we fall. In the stories of Scripture and tradition we see writ large not only the heights but also (and probably more often) the depths of what it is to be human. At its best religion wrestles honestly with the messiness and complexity of who we are and how we might work creatively with that reality.

In the story of the good Samaritan I recognize my capacity not only for the compassion of the Samaritan, but also for the wrong priorities of the priest and Levite, the woundedness of the victim and the self-centred violence of the muggers who take from others what is not theirs, caring nothing about the consequences for their victims. Perhaps it is not surprising that for most of my life I have been moved by, and focused on, the compassion of the Samaritan. Unconsciously I probably found that easier than considering the broken aspects of the other characters. The Samaritan's spontaneous care of the injured man, regardless of how that might put out his schedule or place him at risk of being mugged himself, embodied my own aspirations. In more recent years, painful personal experience has taught me just how hard it is to be truly compassionate: for me it is the greatest challenge of all.

The limits of compassion

The 2013 film *Love is All You Need* tells the story of the love that develops between Philip, a lonely middle-aged widower, and Ida, a married woman recovering from breast cancer. Ida returns home one day to find her husband Leif having sex with a woman the age of their adult daughter. He has been carrying on the affair during Ida's chemotherapy sessions, and is caught *in flagrante* because he hasn't realized those sessions have ended. Leif is completely oblivious to anyone's needs apart from his own. He whines on endlessly about how Ida's illness has impacted upon him just as much as it has her. Leif's total disregard for anyone other than himself stands in sharp contrast to the courage, beauty and self-restraint of Ida. When Leif's exasperated son knocks him down in front of all the guests at a family wedding, many people watching in the cinema cheered, no doubt wondering why no one had thumped this idiot earlier. How could someone be so stupid, so self-centred and so utterly lacking in compassion for his suffering wife? And yet . . .

As a romantic comedy, the film is lightweight. Ida and Leif are stereotypically the 'goodie' who is all good and the 'baddie' who has no redeeming features. The superficiality of the film masks some really important questions about the impact of illness upon not just those who have the illness but also the network of relationships of which they are a part. Compassion depends upon us having the ability to see beyond the superficial, to recognize complexity and even to see that people who may, like Leif, repulse us utterly have a story to tell.

Some years ago there was a news item about a happily married couple. Tragically, the wife was in an accident that left her unconscious and on long-term life support. You can imagine the grief of her husband as he moved from keeping vigil by her bedside to realizing she might not regain consciousness and could be held in this twilight zone of being all-but-dead for who knew how long; her physical presence a constant reminder to him of her absence in every other respect. How hard it must have been for the husband to pick up the pieces of his life and carry on, effectively as a widower. The sense of loneliness and loss must have been overwhelming. As time passed and he worked through his grief he became close to another woman. Then, out of the blue, two years after the accident his wife regained consciousness and made a full recovery.

Suddenly the husband is catapulted back through time, rewinding all his grief; the pieces of his life he had begun to put back together shattering all over again as the beloved one, who was as dead, is now alive to him once more. And what of the love that has blossomed with another woman? The press portrayed the husband as a villain for having developed another relationship during the time his wife was in a coma. They understood how heart-rending it must have been for his wife, coming round to discover that not only had she lost two years of her life in what seemed just like waking up after a night's sleep, but also that her husband had become close to someone else. For the journalist reporting this story she was the 'goodie' and her husband the 'baddie'. But life is far more complicated than that. This was a man who loved his wife and who, having lost her in every respect except for a ventilator and drips keeping her in a basic state of aliveness, was confronted with not knowing if she would ever regain consciousness and, as a result, had to make choices about what to do that none of us would wish to face. At such a traumatic time when, understandably, he most needed the comfort of another person's arms around him, he was condemned for finding new love when his beloved had been taken from him. From the newspaper's point of view, the facts indicated that the man's wife was alive so any relationship he developed with anyone else was adultery.

If you are a person of faith you may agree that condemnation was the only valid response, or you may, like me, feel a different response was needed.

Codes of conduct and caring for humanity

As a practising Jew, Jesus was part of a community in which faithfulness to God was equated with keeping the religious law. There was much debate and disagreement in his community about these laws and what it meant to keep them. Jesus was clear that the law was there to enable the well-being of humanity. The laws concerning the Sabbath came into being to make sure that people took a rest from their labours, and to prevent the exploitation of workers, but they could be taken to extremes. When Jesus healed a man with a withered hand on the Sabbath he scandalized the more legalistic members of his community but he was clear that 'The Sabbath was made for man, not man for the Sabbath'.

The story is also told of a woman who was ritually unclean because she had continuous menstrual bleeding, or maybe she was bleeding as a result of sexual violation. The story isn't specific. All we're told is that she had been bleeding for 12 years. Then she touched Jesus' cloak and was healed. Her action made Jesus ritually unclean but that did not matter to him. It was far more important that the woman was made well. Time and again in the Gospels Jesus makes it clear that compassion supersedes religious legal requirements that have come to dehumanize rather than rehumanize people.

The challenge of compassion

Because compassion often takes us from the clarity of black and white thinking into recognizing shades of grey, it can be a challenge to those of us who don't want to feel discomforted by uncertainty. Just as the words and actions of Jesus challenged those who preferred to see life in clear-cut terms despite the damage that did to people who were struggling, so the demands of compassion today often raise uncomfortable questions about our own uncompromising attitudes. Having held in my early adult life judgemental, dogmatic opinions about what is right, I know these are often rooted in lack of awareness about, or a refusal to acknowledge, personal faults and failings as well as to recognize complexity.

The story about the three people caught up in the gut-wrenching consequences of the wife's long-term coma and unexpected recovery raises difficult questions about relationships, love, marriage, basic human needs, and how all these things interact in the messy experience we call life. How we understand these things is influenced by the attitudes and actions of the key people who are responsible for us through childhood, the things that happen to us as we grow and develop, our personality traits, and our engagement with life beyond our immediate experience. To what extent is our capacity for compassion enabled or eviscerated by these things?

Confronting a personal lack of compassion

Some years ago *The Guardian* featured in their Saturday magazine an article about happily married couples where one of the partners had a chronic, debilitating illness or major disability requiring ongoing daily nursing care. The stories were heart-warming yet I found myself reading them in a state of numbness. None reflected my own experience of living with a chronically ill partner. The disparity between what I read and what I wrestled with myself was such that years later I still remember the feature, the reaction it provoked in me and my sense of having failed miserably to be consistently compassionate with the one person who had the most right to expect that from me.

As a nurse and, later, a priest, I have always had the reputation for being a deeply compassionate person. I can understand why others see me in this way, but I know the reality is much more complicated. When I was offered a place at Florence Nightingale's famous School of Nursing in St Thomas's Hospital, London, I went with the intention of becoming the best nurse since the Lady of the Lamp tended the wounded of Crimea. How naive was I!

It was David who first showed me the complexity of motives behind my desire to care for others. He was admitted to the ward early one afternoon. I was a third-year student nurse and in charge on that shift. David had a deep-vein thrombosis (DVT) and required complete bed rest. Any moving around could dislodge the blood clot in his leg, leading to further and potentially fatal complications. David was also a drug addict in need of his next fix. He was agitated and in no frame of mind to stay in hospital, let alone in bed. He was desperate for a cigarette but smoking in the bays was not allowed. The three other patients around him were all on oxygen so a sneaky fag could be highly explosive as well as unpleasant for them. For about three hours until the doctor I'd bleeped finally managed to make it to the ward, I was constantly back and forth to David, talking quietly, reiterating why he needed to stay in bed, lifting him back into bed when he tried to get out, explaining why smoking wasn't an option and confirming repeatedly that, yes, the doctor had been called and would be with us as soon as other demands allowed. It was exhausting for both of us.

Seeing the wood for the trees

When the doctor finally arrived I had a few minutes' breathing space to reassess the situation. David would be calmer once he had the medication he needed. What, I wondered, could I do to help him engage more easily with the treatment he required? This was not about a battle of wills and one or other of us winning out. We needed to work together. In the end I pushed David's bed into the day room where he could smoke – this being in the days before smoking inside public spaces became illegal. Finally seeing I was on his side and trying to help, he calmed down and began to talk about his unhappy life.

I was deeply grateful for the way in which David opened my eyes to an important insight about why I had chosen to be a nurse. He rattled me because, unlike every other patient I'd looked after until that point, he didn't need me. He needed only his next fix. His withdrawal symptoms were so over-riding that the DVT was inconsequential in comparison, as were my attempts to care for him. My response to his lack of gratitude made me conscious of my own need to be needed. It was what gave me my sense of identity and feeling of worth. Initially unaware of this I had allowed myself to get into loggerheads with David because he was not giving me what I needed. Only when I'd been able to take a little time out had I seen the obvious and was able to stop my own needs getting in the way.

Being wounded healers

Discovering my need to be needed was an important step forward in my development as a nurse and as a human being. Our motives for doing most things are often mixed. That's how it is. It isn't a problem just so long as we have some sense of what drives us. There was a connection between the compassion I felt for my patients and the way in which their need of me fulfilled my own need to be needed. Our relationship was mutually beneficial. I am often moved by the stories of suffering

I hear, whether or not I can do anything about them, but in my early days as a nurse my compassion was fuelled by the need others had of me, and the sense of fulfilment that came with being able to help them in some way or other. David's lack of need for me meant that I had to work much harder to respond compassionately to him. To put it more graphically, it took more effort to *conspire* with him. 'Conspire' comes from the Latin meaning 'to breathe with'. In other words, compassion is about being able to get inside the being of another, to feel their rhythms, to understand how easy it is to catch breath, lose it, feel suffocated or breathe easily in their position. In this context I had to put aside my own need to be needed in order to find a healing way forward for David.

Whether or not we are able to feel compassion and act compassionately depends upon whether or not the needs of the different people in the encounter are complementary or conflicting. When my need synchronized with the needs of my patients compassion overflowed, but that same need could in other situations where it clashed with the needs of others make it much harder for me to feel and act with compassion. The place that has most challenged my sense of being a compassionate person is in my closest relationships.

Questions

1 How do the characters in the story of the good Samaritan play out in your own psyche and experience?
2 Where do you experience the limits of your own compassion?

10

The cost of caring

The story is told of a passer-by offering to help a boy carrying an injured child along the road. 'He ain't heavy, he's my brother,' was the boy's response. As early as the 1920s, those words were taken up by various children's charities. In the 1960s, Bobby Scott and Bob Russell turned them into the song made famous by The Hollies. For the boy who first spoke the words, caring wasn't a burden because the child he carried was family. I can recognize the truth of that in some of my experience, but more frequently than I'd like to admit I have found the opposite to be true.

Charity begins at home?

Families have much stronger expectations and needs of one another, whether spoken or unspoken, than they have of strangers. It took me years to recognize my need for those closest to me to be fit and well. I work a great deal with pain and suffering in other people's lives, and I need a space where all is well and my own pain and suffering can be safely held and worked through. I end up asking my family to be what I would not demand of anyone else, and know I am incapable of myself. Although it was not Jesus' intention in the parable of the good Samaritan to suggest it was easier for the Samaritan, the outsider, to respond to the mugged man than it was for the other two men who were members of the victim's own 'tribe', in the light of my personal struggles that aspect has struck me more recently.

My family tease me about how unsympathetic I am when they are poorly. I followed very much in my mother's footsteps in sending my children to school if they didn't have a temperature and looked fine, regardless of how unwell they said they were feeling. I've always been intolerant when they behave like 'drama queens'.

When my son came home from gymnastics complaining his foot was painful, but then proceeded to bounce up and down on the trampoline, I didn't take his complaint too seriously. When he came back from school the next day using a single crutch, I paused for thought, but watching him run up and down stairs decided that, at worst, his foot was probably only bruised. When he returned from school the following day on two crutches I finally took him to the minor injuries unit. I was mortified to learn he had broken a bone in his foot.

Stiff-upper-lip syndrome

Talking with other nurses I suspect it is a hazard of the job that having worked with seriously ill people, many of whom cope with great fortitude, we tend not to make a big deal of minor ailments and accidents. It is also part of my family 'inheritance' not to make a fuss. Whereas illness or need in people who are not my family brings out the best in me, illness in those closest to me can trigger the worst of reactions. I identify with St Paul in his letter to the Romans, 'I do not understand my own actions. For I do not do what I want, but I do the very thing I hate.'

I need to qualify this statement a little. When the children are obviously ill, I come into my own. When they were little I decamped with them into the guest-room double bed and tended them through the night. I think the comfort of Mummy being close was as important a factor in their recovery as any medicine they took. Being there for my children when they were genuinely sick really mattered to me. That's what mums are for. It goes with the territory of being a parent. In other words, it is what I expected to do as they grew up.

Caring for a chronically ill husband, on the other hand, was not what I expected when I met, fell in love with and married Chris. I know I promised to love him 'in sickness and in health' but frankly, as a 22-year-old, I didn't really think through what that might mean. If I gave potential ill health any consideration at all, it was to see it as something that might happen a long way off in old age and, if my experience so far was anything to go by, I expected to nurse Chris with the same care and compassion I gave to my patients. In reality, my unconscious need was for him to be everything that is the opposite of illness.

To complicate things further, when I understand what is wrong with someone I am able to work with that much more easily than when the diagnosis is uncertain. When Chris became chronically ill with a condition all the consultants took seriously but none could diagnose clearly, I connected more with feelings of frustration and resentment than with compassion. More recently, when a scan revealed a lump in his chest I was better able to cope with the potential diagnosis of cancer than the less definable illness that had impacted so much upon us as a couple and as a family. If it was cancer it would be treatable, containable or terminal and I'd know what I was dealing with. Knowledge empowers me. Lack of knowledge and the sense of helplessness that comes with that are far harder for me to live with. His chronic illness was not only less comprehensible, but the constant pain that came with it meant that while Chris was often physically present he was psychologically absent.

In response to all this, I found my compassion was obliterated by feelings of sadness, anger, frustration and downright self-pity. Guilt at responding badly to him when he couldn't help being unwell made me feel even worse. The grief, of course, was inevitable. His pain meant he couldn't be all I needed him to be. Times of celebration like Christmas sometimes emphasized the unhappiness rather than alleviated it, because he felt less able to enter into the spirit of it than when he had been well.

Crushed by lack of compassion

For his part, Chris felt rejected and isolated. He was carrying on heroically doing the best he could when what he really needed to do was nothing at all, and I was giving him a hard time for something he couldn't help. It seemed so unfair to him. Understandably so! He also felt awful for the impact his illness had on me and the children. Once, when I'd gone out for a drink with my daughter who is eight years older than her brother, we were talking about Chris's illness. Suddenly she burst into tears because she said she felt so sorry that Tian would not experience the 'well daddy' she had grown up with. Being a deeply caring and sensitive man Chris could see all this, even if we tried to downplay the impact of his illness on us all.

Chronic illness provoked in Chris and me reactions we didn't expect and certainly wouldn't choose to feel. But, unbidden, they reared their ugly heads and we had to learn to deal with them. The lessons have been emotionally costly. Sometimes to love each other in this situation is simply not to run away from it. We hang on in, surviving rather than thriving. In our worst moments, thankfully few in number, we have both felt that a more preferable option would be for Chris to die. At those times the thought of being out of pain trumps any other priority for Chris, while for me the possibility of release from all the limitations his illness brings, and the chance to re-engage fully with life instead of feeling caught in suspended animation like an insect in amber, is a more bearable option than the depths we're living through at those points in time. For both of us to acknowledge these things can feel hellish, but it is part of the territory of long-term illness when this explodes into a partnership. Were there not so much love and commitment between us, we might not still be together.

Shared struggle

I talked about this experience with the presenter Chris Evans during one of my Radio 2 'Pause for Thought' slots on his breakfast show. Before I left the studio emails had arrived from listeners living with chronically sick partners. They were thanking me for articulating their experience. Suddenly they felt less lonely and isolated and, in one case, able to talk more honestly and helpfully with their spouse than had previously been possible.

There are no easy answers to living with long-term illness in a partner. Deeply negative reactions are understandable. In this context compassion may not be something that feels lovely or fulfilling. It may not mean responding with warmth and generosity to the one who is sick. It may simply be manifest in a person sticking with a situation that cannot be changed, no matter how much of a struggle that may sometimes be. The nearest a person may get to compassion in this context is to say, 'This is bloody, and we're both struggling, but I will not desert you. We have a history in which we've shared deep love and we're going to hold out. We can't always be what the other needs, but we're both being the best we can be.'

At such times it's important for neither party to beat themselves up psychologically for feeling guilt or grief or all the roller-coaster emotions that are part of the reality of chronic illness. Sometimes it's helpful to talk to kindred spirits in the same situation because they know how tough it can be, and they've long ago dropped the 'oughts' and 'shoulds' and 'have tos' that pepper the advice of people who don't know the experience first-hand. One of the things I'm slowly learning is that when we wrestle honestly with the experience of ill health, either in ourselves or in someone close to us, it can teach us a depth of compassion and humanity that eludes those who know only good health. In fact, I think this is true across the board of human limitations of any kind.

Strength out of weakness

Over the years I have worked hard to understand the needs I have, and to work with them in ways that prevent them sabotaging my private and professional life. I haven't always succeeded in that task. To face my fragility of being when I really want to be a strong leader isn't easy. Yet I'm also conscious that the more I've come to terms with personal inadequacy, failure and uncertainty, the more I've been able to empathize with others who, like me, sometimes find themselves as 'the shuffler in the queue/Holding out his bowl', rather than the one helping to save struggling humanity from self-destruction. The older I get, the more I conclude that if I am compassionate in any way it is not because I am good – far from it – but because I know my own capacity for self-deceit, selfishness and inhumanity.

All this makes me wonder why the Church is insistent on describing Jesus as both fully human *and* without sin, as if God cannot be fleshed out in the lives of imperfect human beings. The opposite is true in my experience. Deeply imperfect people have been a key channel of divine grace for me. I don't need Jesus to have been perfect for him to embody 'God'. When it comes to compassion, can observation ever give anything other than 'outsider' knowledge? Can compassion be inspired (breathed in), or is it expired (breathed out), as a result of the everyday personal deaths we experience when we conspire with all that it means to be human?

Many people find comfort in times of struggle in the image of the crucified Christ. He becomes a fellow sufferer, but he suffers as a victim of the abuse of others. How can he hold my pain as a perpetrator of inhumanity in any meaningful way, if that is beyond his own experience? Did he only mix with sinners and outcasts because he wanted to heal them, or because he felt a kinship with them and knew, as I do, that it is often those who have fallen farthest and have come through whose 'cup runneth over' with compassion? Compassion cannot be manufactured. You can't make it happen. It is a by-product of something else, namely a deep understanding of what it is to be human in all its many shades.

Developing compassion

It should be clear from what I've said so far that coming to terms with personal complexity and mess is one way in which we become more compassionate. Knowing my 'self' can help me to become selfless. It should be equally clear that who we are can also get in the way of becoming compassionate. The self can be deeply selfish. That's one reason why the major faith traditions advocate putting the self to one side. Self-absorption blocks awareness of others. Paradoxically, the more we put selfish needs aside and become open to the needs of others, the more our personal needs are met. But this requires conscious intent and discipline.

Self-giving love

When I spent eight days in Auschwitz concentration camp with a group of Jews, Christians, Hindus and Buddhists some of the Jewish members were survivors or the children of those who had died in or survived the camps, some of the German Christians were the children of camp guards. Each morning we sat in a circle in Auschwitz Birchenau, where the camp guards sent new arrivals getting off the trains, either one way to the gas chambers or the other way to slave labour. We were joined by an elderly man called Marian. As we took it in turns to recite the names of those who had died, their age and country of origin, Marian sat quietly with his wife – his 'angel' as he called her.

Marian was just 17 years old when, as a Polish Roman Catholic, he was sent in one of the first transports to Auschwitz, where he remained for the duration of the war. The number tattooed on his arm was 432. One morning, after sabotage was uncovered in the camp, the guards called all the prisoners out on roll call and demanded that those responsible come forward. No one did, of course, so ten men were picked at random to be sent to the starvation cells. One man, who knew his wife and children were still alive, wept bitterly. Another prisoner, a Franciscan priest called Maximilian Kolbe, stepped out from the greater crowd and asked to take his place. Kolbe died a couple of weeks later in the punishment block after his heart was injected with phenol. The man whose place he had taken survived, as did his family.

Watching this terrible drama unfolding, Marian knew he could not do what Kolbe had done: he could not give his life for someone he did not know, but he resolved to live with as much humanity as his survival allowed. One day he stopped himself dragging a body from the gas chamber to the ovens. Wasted as he was, he picked up the body and carried it with dignity to be cremated. It was his closest friend. He tried where possible to share his rations. He carried the bowls of those too weak to carry their own: to lose one's bowl was a death sentence.

When liberation came Marian went on to become a well-known stage-set designer. For 50 years he remained silent about his experiences in Auschwitz. Then, in his seventies, he had a stroke. To help restore movement in his partially paralysed arm his doctors encouraged him to draw. Marian found the only images he could put on paper were his memories of Auschwitz as they had percolated in his mind over the years. For two years he drew compulsively; his pictures a haunting and harrowing legacy not only of what happened in Auschwitz but also the psychological nightmare of living with the memories.

Marian was in his eighties when I met him on the selection ground. One evening we joined him to see the permanent exhibition of his paintings in the Franciscan church three kilometres from the camp. Here we were able to talk with him as we had not been able to do during the silences in the camp. He was the most humble, humane and humorous man I have had the privilege to meet. He spoke about living with the legacy of his experiences in Auschwitz and the unanswered questions he had, and wondered if we might have answers. We did not.

One of the Jewish women in the group had explored Kabbalistic thought (Jewish mystical tradition). She said numbers had particular meanings and, referring to the number tattooed on Marian's arm, she said 4 stood for the four directions (north, south, east and west) and 32 denoted a full heart. For her, the number imposed on Marian to dehumanize him had become the number that symbolized his deepest humanity, a full heart overflowing in all directions.

Marian's compassion began with a realistic but profound commitment to be as mindful of his fellow prisoners as was possible in the utterly dehumanizing circumstances in which he was forced to live in Auschwitz. In that terrible place he consciously tried to hold the tension between his own survival and that of his fellow sufferers, to be humane in the midst of soul-destroying inhumanity. He has tried to practise that all his life. His capacity for compassion is hard won.

In his first letter to the Corinthians, St Paul talks about how he and the people he's addressing 'see through a glass darkly', but when the kingdom of God comes they will see 'face to face'. The distinction between seeing as one might when looking into a polished metal mirror and seeing face to face captures an important psychological truth. Because of our different needs and neuroses, when we think we're relating to others what we may be relating to are aspects of our own selves with which we may or may not have come to terms. In other words when we look at another we see a reflection of who we are. If we do not understand it for what it is, this reflection can prevent us from truly seeing the other who stands before us, face to face. We cannot recognize a reflection unless we know who is being reflected, in other words, unless we know ourselves.

Living with limitations

I'm struggling here for the right words because I'm not sure if I am capable of feeling compassion for aspects of another's experience that are alien to me. I need some point of connection, and I need also to acknowledge that while I want to make room for the human stories of others, I am not always going to understand what they have lived through because it is their experience and not mine. There is a difference between having a good sense of judgement and being judgemental about another. The former relies on deep knowing, whereas the latter comes from knowing about, but not knowing. The former relies on intimate contact, the latter looks on from a distance.

In this muddle I am clear about one thing: our capacity for compassion is not dependent upon us being good, but upon how we understand our brokenness and work with the sometimes crucifying experiences that are part of life. There are no easy answers in this. Compassion is costly, and we are all at different stages of understanding what it is and how we might make room for it in our lives. When we encounter the absence of compassion in others, compassion demands that we remember our own incapacity for it and bear in mind what has helped us to a deeper understanding. We can take hope from the fact that when we feel most fragile, conscious of our faults and failings, it is often then that we are closest to becoming compassionate, as Naomi Shihab Nye expresses in her poem 'Kindness'.

Kindness

Before you know what kindness really is,
you must lose things,
feel the future dissolve in a moment
like salt in a weakened broth.
What you held in your hand,
what you counted and carefully saved,
all this must go so you know
how desolate the landscape can be
between the regions of kindness.
How you ride and ride
thinking the bus will never stop,
the passengers eating maize and chicken
    will stare out the window forever.

Before you learn the tender gravity of kindness,
you must travel where the Indian in a white poncho
lies dead by the side of the road.
You must see how this could be you,
how he too was someone
who journeyed through the night with plans
and the simple breath that kept him alive.

Before you know kindness as the deepest thing inside,
you must know sorrow as the other deepest thing.
You must wake up with sorrow.
You must speak it till your voice
catches the thread of all sorrows
and you see the size of the cloth.

Then it is only kindness that makes sense anymore,
only kindness that ties your shoes
and sends you out into the day to mail letters and
    purchase bread,

only kindness that raises its head
from the crowd of the world to say
it is I you have been looking for,
and then goes with you every where
like a shadow or a friend.[1]

In this section the stories I've told speak of personal conflict, within me and, often as a result of that, with others. Dealing well with conflict is difficult, so let's turn our attention to that subject after the questions below.

Questions

1 In your experience, what does compassion look like?
2 How does your degree of compassion for others compare with your degree of compassion for yourself?

Part 5

CONFLICT

11

No peace in our time

I am sitting in the home of a Palestinian Muslim family in a restricted area of Hebron in the West Bank. We are gathered around a small table in the living room, eating an evening meal of bread, olives, tomatoes, dips and fruit. I am a little distracted. As we eat, large rocks are ricocheting off the barred windows, rattling down on the flat roof of this one-storey house and crashing on the ground outside. My friends, Hasham and Nisreen, their two primary-age children and young baby carry on as if nothing is happening. The settlers who live opposite have stoned their home many times before, and worse. The barrage goes on for an hour. The police are called but do not come. Neither do the army. Eventually, a representative of the Red Cross takes down the details. The provocation for this attack seems to be the fact that Hasham has had three international groups visit him today to hear about his family's experience of living under the Occupation. The second group prompted a number of Israeli soldiers to take up positions in the olive grove below the house. When I looked down on them over the garden wall they were all on one knee along its length, their guns pointing in the direction of where we would walk when we returned the visitors to the checkpoint. While the third group were with us, the soldiers came up to the house. Hasham and Nisreen went out to meet them. I sat quietly on the wall beside them. Hasham held a copy of the Geneva Convention on Human Rights. After a brief conversation the soldiers left. An hour later the rocks began hitting the house.

I am not only unnerved by the experience of being stoned but I also feel profound anger at the injustices I witness and hear about during my stay. I have much to learn from the fortitude, courage and quiet steadiness displayed by Hasham as he continues to work for peace while experiencing the daily humiliations and violent attacks that go with refusing to leave the home his family has lived in for generations.

A few years on, while working on this chapter, news comes of Palestinian and Israeli representatives meeting in Washington to begin conversations about potential peace talks. We've been here before. Few people I know hold out any hope of resolution. Violent conflict is the way of the Middle East, they say. Syria is in the midst of a bloody civil war. Egypt teeters on the edge of one. Bombs continue to go off in Iraq and Afghanistan.

'Why can't they sort themselves out?' asks one incredulous acquaintance. Implicit in his question is the assumption that 'they' are not like 'us'. 'We' would never end up in such a situation. He has little awareness about the part we played in creating these conflicts. By distancing himself from the atrocities he hears are happening, he takes a step towards the very violence of which he thinks he is incapable. To think we are not as other human beings is a real Achilles heel.

Samson's delusion

In the biblical book of Judges is another man who thinks he is a cut above the rest, unsullied by the limitations of lesser mortals. His name is Samson. His story might be described as a testosterone-fuelled existence writ large. He takes and discards women without thought for them or their families, and he thinks nothing of killing thousands when he feels his own honour has been slighted. His strength is super-human. As a result, so the story goes, he is one of the Judges of Israel for 20 years. His arrogance – or is it a lack of emotional intelligence? – is his ultimate downfall. He falls in love with Delilah who works for his enemies, the Philistines. She coaxes out from him the source of his unnatural strength – his hair. His hair? If you find your incredulity stretched to breaking point, please bear with me. Delilah shaves off Samson's hair while he sleeps, and he wakes to find his power gone. The Philistines take him, gouge out his eyes, shackle and imprison him and, at a time of feasting, force him to entertain them like some kind of performing animal.

Dehumanizing others

The legendary story of Samson, like any archetypal story, contains powerful symbolism that cuts to the core of human experience. That Samson's strength lies in his hair is heart-achingly insightful, as I learnt when I visited Auschwitz. On the first floor of one of the barrack huts is the hair memorial. About a third of this upper floor is sectioned off by a glass wall that runs the length of the dormitory. Behind the glass lies human hair piled up to waist height and above. This is the hair shaved from the heads and bodies of the men, women and children who were sent to Auschwitz to die in its gas chambers or to be worked to death as slave labourers. I stand looking at this tragic testimony to the humanity of the victims and the inhumanity of those who shaved them, physically winded by the sight of it. I'm conscious of my own hair, which hangs down to the top of my thighs. I remember how, as I grew it long, I was overwhelmed by the sense I was growing into my own identity.

For the Nazis, shaving the heads and bodies of those arriving in the camps was one way of stripping away their identity, of dehumanizing them. When we dehumanize others we disempower them. We take away their strength and diminish their being. We see them as 'not us'. The more psychological distance we create between 'us' and 'them' the easier it is to perpetrate violence against them. That's one of the things the story of Samson articulates.

It is worth remembering that Samson's last act is an act of revenge that kills not only those who have brought about his downfall but also himself. There are few winners in the cycles of violence, fuelled by acts of vengeance, into which we fall. Even the victors are casualties, and the legacy of conflict goes on long after the violence has ceased.

Humility vs humiliation

'Humility' and 'humiliate' are similar words with very different meanings. Humility is the quality we have when we have a modest opinion of our own importance, keeping our sense of self in perspective. It is an attribute. To be humiliated is to have our human dignity undermined by others and to be seen as less than we are. It is an abuse. Humility humanizes us. Humiliation dehumanizes us. Humiliation is a characteristic of conflict. Being rehumanized, in our own eyes and in the eyes of others, is part of the process of healing as we work with the legacy of conflict.

Thankfully, for many of us in the West violent conflict is not part of our first-hand experience, but being with men and women in communities experiencing or emerging from violent conflict I have learnt that the human dynamics we see writ large in their lives are the same in the lesser conflicts most of us deal with on a day-to-day basis. We may not shave the heads of those with whom we are at odds, for example, but how often do we dehumanize others in our language. 'He's a pig!' 'She's a bitch!' 'They're idiots!' We may not resort to physical violence but we are as capable of taking sides, being at loggerheads, wanting others to suffer for the suffering they've caused us, and, to varying degrees, being both victims and perpetrators of inhumanity. Here again there may be a gap between what we publicly aspire to and what we privately struggle with. We may want to live in peace but somehow our capacity for conflict gets in the way. No, that's not quite right. It is our inability to deal with conflict that frequently gets in the way. This inability is often rooted in an inaccurate assumption that conflict is by definition bad and to be avoided.

The elephant in the room

I have no memory of my parents arguing. I grew up in a happy secure family. Of course, I inevitably fell out with my sisters and brother, and I found that distressing. As the youngest I always seemed to lose! I do remember times when I was afraid of my father's anger. At some point in my childhood I came to associate being loved with being in agreement with those who loved me. When I did something wrong and was chastised for it, I felt love had been withdrawn. I could deal with arguments if I was in a specific role, like that of sports team captain, Head Girl or Guide Patrol Leader, and I was not part of the argument. Otherwise I was fearful of conflict and tried to avoid it or appease the people involved. If I upset my parents I often scribbled little notes of apology after I'd been sent to bed and left them by their bed. When things went wrong my default position was to behave as if it was my fault. Conflict wasn't something we were taught to expect and work with. As Christians I rather think we considered conflict to be a sign of failure and I don't ever remember us talking about it in any healthy kind of way.

Other people grow up surrounded by family conflict and the breakdown of relationships. Their memory is of parents fighting and people shouting at rather than speaking to one another. Or else they remember long silences pregnant with unspoken anger, frustration and disagreement. They experienced conflict but they didn't see it resolved well. Like me they may well have left home equally ill-equipped to deal with it.

Conflict and identity

When I ask participants in workshops what comes to mind when I say the word conflict, more often than not the replies are of negative images. This shared perception is profoundly damaging to human well-being. Conflict is an inevitable and potentially positive part of life. At its most basic, conflict may be defined as difference plus tension. The degree to which we experience the tension depends upon the degree to which our identity is threatened by the different ideas, encounters and experiences that come our way. For example, people of different genders, sexual orientations, racial backgrounds and religious creeds can and do work well together. Those differences are not in themselves necessarily a cause of conflict. They only become so when a person's identity feels threatened by the differences. The threat may be real or imagined. If imagined, the conflict will say more about the inner psychological landscape of the person feeling threatened than it does about those who are perceived as a threat.

Since our sense of identity is shaped by what we already know, new information that challenges our understanding and our sense of self will provoke conflicting thoughts and feelings. These are a normal part of the process of becoming wiser. It's rather like jumping from one stepping stone to another. There's a point when you land on the new stone and wobble as you find your balance. You're going forward, but taking the leap can be unnerving and until you land and regain your balance you may not be entirely sure about the strength of your new position.

Even when we are open to new ways of seeing and being, the challenges these bring may leave us feeling very conflicted. I was acutely aware of this many years ago when I began working with colleagues from other faiths or speaking with thoughtful atheist friends. They asked questions that fellow Christians didn't generally think to ask because we shared the same assumptions. Their thoughtful questions challenged my certainties and proved profoundly unsettling because I found my understanding to be inadequate in the light of them. Like Eve I was cast out of the Eden of my comfort zone and had to radically rethink my position and discover an identity that didn't require certainty of outlook in order to feel secure.

Security in uncertainty

Security is an important factor. The greater the insecurity in our lives, the more many of us need some rock of certainty on which to cling. People often associate certainty with truth, but I've come to agree with Morgan Scott Peck's assessment that 'We are most in the dark when we are the most certain, and the most enlightened when we are the most confused.'[1]

My rabbi friend, Professor Jonathan Magonet, reminded me that when Moses went up the mountain to meet with God he always ended up lost in a cloud! In his absence his people in the valley far below built a golden calf because they needed something solidly certain to worship as they wandered around the wilderness learning what it meant to be the people of Israel, no longer slaves but free. We're told they were in the desert for 40 years, about the time it took for the generation who had been slaves to die. It's hard to relinquish the different thoughts, feelings and behaviours that enslave us and to be open to new ways of understanding and acting. That's why, ultimately, positive change often comes with conflict.

One well-known defence against embracing necessary change is to claim that this is how things have always been. The evidence of history indicates otherwise. 'We often take for granted that things have always been like this, but . . . to understand the past is to understand how things change.'[2] Just because a particular perspective has been long-held does not make it right. For centuries people in England believed that swans could only ever be white and then, when they landed in Australia, they discovered swans could be black as well.

Being right and the numbers game

Sometimes we claim that our certainties must be correct because the majority of people are on our side of the argument, but those who have made new discoveries or taken a stand against injustice have, at first, often been lone voices 'crying in the wilderness'. The masses welcoming Hitler at the Nuremberg rallies were clearly wrong in supporting a regime responsible for the Holocaust. Think, too, of the minority voices crying out for justice at the beginning of protests against slavery and apartheid and in support of votes for women. They were initially denounced by the majority. Challenging the status quo can be costly.

Into this melting pot we must also add the impact of our capacity both to wound and to be wounded. In situations of violent conflict we talk about 'victims' and 'perpetrators', the ones to whom violence has been done and the ones responsible for the violence. The terms are problematic, but looking at some of the problems around them can help us understand further reasons why, whatever our desire for a peaceful existence or to deal well with our differences, we end up in destructive conflict. Before going on, take a little time to reflect on the following questions.

Questions

1 What did you learn about conflict and how to deal with it during your childhood?
2 What do you understand by the terms 'victim' and perpetrator'?
3 What have you felt when you were a victim or perpetrator?

12

Faith in conflict

———◆•◆•◆———

Few of us choose to become a victim. Who would want to be one? Some who are victims of another person's or group's harmful action either do not use, or quickly relinquish, the term 'victim' because it defines them according to what someone else has done to them. They prefer to speak of themselves as a 'survivor' because that shows they are defining who they are according to their own decisions and refusing to be 'at the mercy' of the one who has forced upon them an unwelcome psychological relationship through the violations committed. Or perhaps there's more to being a victim than that.

Few of us see ourselves as perpetrators. When we take action to the detriment of others we may justify our actions, seeing ourselves as doing the 'right' thing. Perpetrators are other people, not me. Or perhaps there's more to being a perpetrator than that.

The politics of the terms 'victim' and 'perpetrator'

As a victim I may feel disempowered by the actions of the perpetrator and believe that it is up to others to make things better for me because I am, after all, the victim. In reality, while we may well need the help and support of other people we can only become survivors or be among those who stand tall if we cease to see ourselves as victims and choose to embrace a different identity. This changing the way we see ourselves may be something we have to keep doing minute by minute, hour by hour, day by day, because the hurt we've experienced runs deep, which is why it can feel more manageable to hold on to the identity of 'victim'. I've done that myself and I know from experience that in so doing I took over from the person who originally hurt me in perpetuating my pain. 'It's your fault that I feel as I do,' I say, but once I acknowledge what has been done and how I feel, I have some choice about how I respond.

These words are easily said but sometimes very difficult to live. When I've been most hurt it has felt like I don't have any choice at all. At such times I recall the words of the psychiatrist Viktor Frankl, who was a prisoner in Auschwitz:

We who lived in concentration camps can remember the men who walked through the huts comforting others, giving away their last piece of bread. They may have been few in number, but they offer sufficient proof that everything can be taken from a man but one thing: the last of the human freedoms – to choose one's attitude in any given set of circumstances, to choose one's own way.[1]

In an earlier chapter I spoke about Marian, a prisoner in Auschwitz who made a conscious choice to live with as much humanity as he could while trying to ensure his survival.

His extreme story movingly illustrates choices made in the face of the inhumanity of others, but its truths are equally relevant to our usually less extreme challenges. His example encourages me to stand tall and carry on, but, if I'm honest, it doesn't necessarily take away the anguish of unresolved psychological pain.

When I am the one who has got things wrong and perpetrated harm I also have difficult choices to make. I'm reminded of the experience of my friend and teacher, Alistair, when he was released from the Maze prison after 12 years. At the age of 17, as a Loyalist paramilitary, he had shot dead a Republican in a revenge attack. Prison gave him the opportunity to reflect on the violence he'd lived through growing up in the Northern Ireland conflict, and his understanding changed radically. In the eyes of others this change was irrelevant. *He's a murderer, the scum of the earth. Nothing changes that.* When you meet constantly with the condemnation and rejection of others who see you as you *were*, rather than as you *are* now, it's hard not to get caught up again in the feelings of anger, fear, hatred and aggression that for many years were your default emotional position.

Not long after his release from the Maze, Alistair was invited to speak to members of a Victims' Support Group. On arrival it turned out his audience had not been made aware of his history. When they were told about it they refused to eat with him and he was forced to have lunch outside. Waiting while the group determined what would happen next, Alistair felt furious and profoundly vulnerable. To come with his background to speak to such a group took immense courage and the response of the group left him feeling, *Fuck it! What's the point. I might as well give up now and go home.* But another 'voice' in his mind counselled differently. *You knew this was going to be tough. The reactions of the group are understandable. Nothing will change unless you remain committed to having these difficult conversations. You can't walk away when things like this happen.*

In the end the group agreed to hear him out, although they decided they would not be asking him any questions at the end. However, when he finished speaking some of his listeners did want to ask questions. They talked for an hour. It was tough for everyone, but in that conversation connections developed between Alistair and some of his audience which continued after he went home that day. When the tensions in the Province were particularly bad again, one of the group, whose husband had been killed by Loyalist paramilitaries in the organization to which Alistair had belonged, rang him to ask if he was OK.[2]

Choosing our attitudes and actions in the face of the ongoing inhumanity of others, or when we have hurt others and are condemned or rejected by them, takes not only courage but huge amounts of emotional energy. It would be far easier in the moment to allow our own humanity to be destroyed by the inhumanity of others and to respond in kind to their condemnation. That's in part why conflict persists. Breaking the patterns and bridging the gulf of understanding between conflicting parties is much harder than maintaining the battle lines.

The power of being a victim

This may be complicated further by a dynamic that isn't easily articulated because it raises uncomfortable questions about those who have been hurt. Alongside the sense of being powerless, or continuing to see ourselves as powerless even when the perpetrator is no longer present, being a victim can also bring with it unexpected power.

In April 2013, planning permission was granted to build a peace centre on part of the site of the former Maze prison, outside Belfast in Northern Ireland. In the following months there was increasing concern expressed about this by various victims'/survivors' groups. This was taken very seriously by the media who seemed to feel the project should not go ahead because of the unhappiness expressed about it by these groups. I could understand this position so I was surprised when a friend challenged me about it.

'Just because my brother was shot dead it doesn't mean I'm any more right than any one who hasn't suffered loss in this conflict. I want you to be sensitive to my experience but don't assume that my opinion, or that of any other victim of the Troubles, is wiser because of the grief and loss we've experienced. These things can just as easily destroy our humanity as deepen it.'

I've learnt from other friends who lived through conflict in different parts of the world that there can be a hierarchy of victimhood with more weight being attached to the views of those who have lost the most relatives, or experienced the most severe injuries as a result of bombings and shootings. This indiscriminate elevation of victims means that when they speak or behave inappropriately they are not always challenged as others without that 'status' would be.

I'm conscious in more day-to-day conflicts at work or home of a similar dynamic sometimes playing out: of people competing to see who is having the toughest time; of there being an expectation of inappropriate special treatment from someone who has been hurt by the words or actions of another; and of someone using their status as a victim to manipulate others. The wounds we have had inflicted on us become the weapons we use against others. In other words, we can move from being the person who has been hurt to becoming the person who causes harm to others.

I often recall a comment made by an old acquaintance, Rabbi Lionel Blue, when he said we will have learnt nothing from the Holocaust until we recognize the Nazi within each of us.

I was reminded of Lionel's words when I spent eight weeks in Israel and the West Bank. I was researching transformative relationships across that conflict divide. During that time I met many amazing Palestinians and Israelis working together and seeking a just solution to the conflict between them. Some were ex-combatants. Some had been bereaved through the actions of the other community and had every reason to hate one another but had come to believe there had to be a way other than that of violence to transform their situation for the well-being of both communities.

My work also involved talking with people from both communities who saw any type of communication between them as an act of betrayal or treason. I was very conscious of one Holocaust survivor who, in the face of the rockets being fired into Israel from Gaza, said he wanted all the Palestinians in Gaza to be washed into the sea or sent to the gas chambers. His response disturbed me greatly. I spoke about it when I met up with a lovely Israeli academic, who regularly protested against injustices being perpetrated against Palestinians and whose area of research was the experience of Holocaust survivors in Israel. How, I asked her, could people who suffered terribly in the Holocaust seek to inflict similar inhumanity on others? Many do not, she countered, but for some people the experience of such horror means that to avoid the possibility of it happening again, they will do whatever they need to, even if that means making others suffer as they have done.

Wolf in sheep's clothing

It was my much-loved son Tian who put me most powerfully in touch with my own potential for violence. He was nine years old at the time. He had been diagnosed with type 1 diabetes a year earlier and was yet to be diagnosed as having attention deficit hyperactivity disorder (ADHD). The combination was sometimes extremely difficult to manage and there were times when I felt defeated by the challenges of it. Our getting-ready-for-school routine, like that in any family, was not the most relaxing. On this particular morning Tian was not in the least bit interested in getting up, sorting out his blood sugar and injection, having breakfast and gathering his school bits together. I began by talking in a quiet, calm voice, but as the minutes ticked by and Tian did nothing without repeated and increasingly heated instruction from me, I began to feel really angry until after 40 minutes I lost it completely. I shouted and banged my fists on the wall. It was as if all the pent-up emotion of the last year, of living with the fear that my son might die of his illness and with my inability to deal sometimes with his challenging behaviour, suddenly spilled over. In that moment not only did I feel I could hurt Tian, I really wanted to. To make sure that didn't happen I put him in the TV room and locked myself in my study until I'd calmed down. I'd succeeded in frightening both of us. I spent a little time hugging and talking with my now co-operative son and then dropped him off at school before going to my first meeting of the day ... on conflict transformation!

My own potential for violence paradoxically came out of my sense of powerlessness in the face of not knowing what to do. I felt like the victim in this scenario, and in response I could so easily have become the perpetrator of physical violence.

The sins of the fathers (and mothers)

Caring for Tian has also helped me to see how we repeat patterns of behaviour through the generations. He has very similar reactions to me when it comes to situations where he doesn't feel in control and he thinks life is conspiring against him. I in turn inherited them from my father and, from what my mother tells me, they were also part of my grandfather's emotional landscape. I suspect my father would not have appreciated being on the receiving end of his father's reactions, just as I found the same reactions hard to cope with in him and Tian finds difficult in me. Aware of these reactions and what provokes them generally speaking means I can keep them in check, but from time to time, when I feel tired or helpless, they explode out and are very unedifying. The writers of the material contained in the books of Exodus and Numbers in the Hebrew Bible speak of the iniquity of the fathers being visited upon the children to the third and fourth generations. Whatever they may have meant by these words it seems to me to be the case that some patterns are deeply ingrained in our collective family psyches and at times when we have lost rational control may emerge to challenge our positive self-image.

Being both victim and perpetrator

The victim/perpetrator dynamic is often far more complicated than we care to admit. Does a person cease to be a victim because, in response to pain he has experienced, he chooses to use violence and become the perpetrator of pain? Is a person who has used violence against others any less a victim when she is maimed by the violence of others? If I have hurt other people less than you have hurt other people does that give me the right to condemn your behaviour more than I condemn my own? How can one measure another person's pain and compare it with the pain of others? Yet, just as there are hierarchies among victims, so it seems there are also hierarchies among perpetrators. Jailed sex offenders, and particularly paedophiles, experience violence at the hands of other prisoners who may well have committed murder but somehow consider their own crime is more acceptable than that of a man who abuses a child. In our own workplaces and home environments most of us are capable of making value judgements about the hurt others cause compared to the hurt for which we are responsible.

In Northern Ireland, when men explain how the maiming or murder of their relatives prompted them down the paramilitary route, they are often met with the response of others saying they too experienced bereavement in the Troubles but did not go on to embrace violence. The latter take the moral high ground. Yet sometimes it is something extraordinarily trivial that determines the path we take. A friend experienced the violence of Bloody Sunday and the loss of friends on that day. In the aftermath he was going to join the IRA. One reason that didn't happen is that the local IRA recruiting officer was out when he turned up at his flat to sign up. It also happened that one of my friend's heroes was English goalkeeper Gordan Banks, whom he was lucky enough to meet. In the light of this meeting he couldn't hold on to the view that the English were all bad. Sometimes the choices we make are due to nothing more than simple circumstances beyond our control.

The choice of evils

Sometimes the choices we have are not between right and wrong but between evils. Either way, someone is going to get hurt and you have to decide which is the lesser of the two evils. I was deeply moved by the story told to me by a Vietnam veteran. I'll call him Jim. He was a young GI on patrol in the jungle when unexpectedly he came across a Vietnamese man asleep in a hammock. The man woke up as Jim approached. For what seemed like an eternity they stared in fear at one another. Then the man reached down into his hammock. Jim assumed he was reaching for a weapon and in the split second he had to decide what to do, he shot him dead. When he went over to check the body he discovered the man had not been reaching for a gun, but for photographs of his family to show Jim. Of all the deaths for which Jim was responsible during the Vietnam war, this death was the one with which he never came to terms.

Like Jim we make our decisions based on what is known to us, just as those who oppose us make their decisions on what is known to them. We are both right according to what we see and understand of the situation, and both wrong according to what we cannot see from where we stand.

Which brings us to an interesting point: in order to get a sense of the whole situation we need the perspective of those we oppose, just as they need ours. Loyalist and Republican ex-paramilitary colleagues tell me that before they met one another they did not consider each other to be human. In the midst of the violence there was no chance of finding out the reality. If they'd met on the street they'd have shot one another given half a chance, but during the peace process, when they finally came together in ex-combatant workshops, they discovered similar stories in the experiences of their enemies and a shared humanity. They didn't, and still don't, necessarily agree with one another politically but through the eyes of the other they have come to see what was not visible from where they once stood.

Choosing to hold the tensions

Allowing your perceptions to be changed, particularly when the understanding you've had has enabled you to justify extreme violence, or when you've lost relatives at the hands of the other person or of their community, takes extraordinary courage. It may well mean that you are rejected or criticized by your own community, who feel betrayed by you. In some instances speaking out against injustice and inhumanity or working for peace can put your life at risk, with death threats coming from your own community as well as that of your enemy. Working for peace, paradoxically, can bring conflict into your life.

One piece of archive footage I saw in Auschwitz was of the local villagers who, when Auschwitz was liberated, were forced to go round the camp, to see the mass graves, the gas chambers and ovens, and to bury the bodies, to see what had happened in their midst. While I cannot imagine ever perpetrating violence against another human being except as a last resort and in self-defence or the defence of my family, I do wonder if I might have been among those millions who did nothing to challenge, prevent or work to overthrow the horror happening within sight of their homes, for fear of what might happen to them or their family.

Reaching out across a conflict divide or challenging abuses is costly. This is also the case in the lesser conflicts and disputes at work or home that most of us get caught up in from time to time. It's the reason why many of us do not take the action we need to take when conflict flares.

Understanding why people do what they do is critically important if we are to deal constructively with conflict. To understand is not to condone. We can understand why a nation renowned for its level of education could embrace the politics of Hitler and rally to his war cry after years of humiliation following the First World War, even though we condemn the horrors of the Holocaust. If we had been more aware of the human dynamics of humiliating people, we might have treated Germany differently after the First World War, but that understanding came too late and we had no choice two decades later but to go to war with the monster we had helped to create.

Peace-building

Avoiding destructive conflict depends upon our capacity to understand the perspective of people with whom we disagree. No one stands where they do without reason – good or bad. Our natural inclination when conflict threatens is to put as much distance as possible between us and those with whom we are at odds, psychologically if not physically, but conflict can only be transformed if we bridge the gap between us and have the difficult conversations that need to be had.

It struck me after one particular visit to Northern Ireland, listening to people from both communities, at grass roots level and in Stormont, that the words attributed to Jesus in the Sermon on the Mount, 'Blessed are the peacemakers for they shall inherit the earth', are extraordinarily challenging: the key peacemakers in any conflict are those who caused and perpetuate the conflict. Unless they become part of the peace process, there can be no lasting peace. By definition, peacemakers must include your enemies. For them the blessing must include you. The inheritance is therefore to be everyone's. That means we need, at some point, to both recognize our potential to be a victim, a perpetrator and the enemy of another, and to relinquish those very same labels in preference to the overarching one of 'peacemaker'. I think that's the hardest thing to do in any conflict, whether it's a major international war or a family or workplace argument. Anglican priest Eric Symes Abbott captures the difficulty in this poem:

How can I love my neighbour as myself
when I need him as my enemy –
when I see in him the self I fear to own
and cannot love?

How can there be peace on earth
while our hostilities are our most
cherished possessions –
defining our identity, confirming
our innocence?[3]

Publicly we speak of wanting to live in peace but privately we find that conflict is a part of life, both for positive reasons and negative, and few of us are equipped to enable its creative possibilities and work with its destructive potential. Publicly we speak of wanting to live in peace, but our experience as people who get hurt and cause harm puts us into conflict, within ourselves and with others. Publicly we speak of wanting to live in peace, but how many of us are prepared to do the work and pay the price that a just peace demands? Publicly we speak of wanting to live in peace, but we have yet to work out how to live peacefully with our own inner complexity and in communities where people want to live in diverse and sometimes diametrically opposed ways.

We may have been lucky enough to avoid armed conflict but there is one area of human experience around which most of us will at some point experience conflict of other kinds. Paradoxically, it is where many of us expect love to be most intimately expressed, namely, sexual expression. That's where our attention will turn after the final questions of this chapter.

Questions

1 What or who provokes violent responses in you?
2 What decisions have you had to make that have involved a choice of evils?
3 What's the difference between wanting peace and being a peacemaker?

Part 6

LOVE AND SEX

13

Only fifty shades of grey?

----•·•◦•·•----

'They're selling *Fifty Shades of Grey* at my local supermarket check-out,' says my lovely friend Alison in mock horror. 'I'd rather be tempted by a Mars bar!'

Alison is no moralizing prude. She's a wonderful and wise woman of the world.

'We've had erotic literature for centuries,' she says, with the authority of one who has read and enjoyed some of it. That said, after decades of women fighting for equality and mutual respect, she like me wonders why a story about a man's sexual domination of a woman should become an international best-seller among a largely female readership, triggering a spike in the sadomasochistic sex-toy market of Ann Summers shops. It seems a retrograde step.

Not that my own sexual fantasies have always been free of the element of domination. I mention this because I think it important to recognize that many of our sexual responses exist irrespective of what we may consciously think is or is not appropriate. I am well aware that what sometimes emerges in the realm of fantasy is the antithesis of what I would want to experience in reality. Many aspects of our sexual identity lie outside our control. The critical thing is what we do with the complexity of who we are as sexual beings, and that we are able to distinguish between what humanizes and rehumanizes us, and what is humiliating and dehumanizing. Sexual dynamics can be every bit as complicated as any other area of human interaction, not least because they are influenced by diverse, sometimes contradictory and not always conscious factors.

In this chapter and the next, I want to look at some of the challenges that have emerged for me around sexual expression and to consider the issues that make this a beautiful aspect of being human, a source of deep pain or a battleground that breaks relationships and causes considerable distress. I am not going to discuss homosexuality as distinct from hetero-sexuality or consider the controversies around the former. It is irrelevant to me whether a relationship is gay or straight. My concern is the love expressed in the relationship and that isn't determined by the sexual orientation of the couple. It's been my joy to witness loving gay and straight relationships, and my sorrow to witness unloving and abusive straight and gay relationships. I affirm love in whatever guise it comes and try to understand the reasons why some relationships are unloving and abusive.

'The woman taken in adultery'

I am rooting this exploration in a well-known story from John's Gospel. It tells how a group of learned men bring to the attention of Jesus a woman who has been caught in the act of adultery, for which the punishment is death by stoning. Interestingly, her 'partner in crime' has not been brought with her. The title of the story is misleading because the woman's sexual conduct is not the significant element of the account. It is the attitudes of the men and the society of which they're a part that concern Jesus. I think it's also true today that our preoccupation with what people get up to in bed says far more about wider inequalities, ignorance, religious neurosis and power issues than it does about sex itself.

When I was working with survivors of sexual violence in the Democratic Republic of the Congo this story held particular resonance. Having become pregnant as a result of rape, sometimes on numerous occasions, the girls and women found themselves rejected by their family and community. As a result of being abandoned some had become prey to other men who gave them a home and had sex with them. In the absence of contraception they inevitably became pregnant again, at which point they were abandoned by the men who'd taken them in. Clearly, alongside the impact of war and poverty, the key issues here are the behaviour of men towards women, the place the former give to the latter in a patriarchal society, and the ethics of a community that blames the woman for a crime committed against her while the rapist goes scot-free.

Using others for our own purposes

The men in John's story want Jesus' opinion about what has happened and the validity of the prescribed penalty. John makes it clear they are using the woman's situation for purposes that have nothing to do with the rights or wrongs of what she has done, and everything to do with testing out, possibly even tricking, Jesus. Now as then, people are prepared to abuse others by taking their human experience and using it either to support their own agenda or to test out or sabotage that of their opponents. The men in John's story have no regard for the sensibilities of the woman, just as in debates today, whether religious, political or otherwise, those arguing may not be appropriately mindful of the people whose personal problems they expose for their own purposes. For example, Channel 4's documentary *Benefits Street* about people living on social benefits stirred up controversy when it was first aired in January 2014, with some suggesting it was nothing more than poor-bashing poverty porn, exploiting already vulnerable people.

Confronted by the men's challenge, Jesus could have responded as we human beings so often do when put on the spot; he could have gone on the defensive, protested against the tactics used or verbally attacked his questioners. It would have been easy to be drawn into the heightened emotion of the men calling for the woman's blood. Instead (to emphasize what I said in an earlier chapter), Jesus remains silent, simply bending down to write with his finger on the ground. Physically he takes the position of weakness as the men stand over him and the woman. He ceases to be a threat. As in many other situations when those around him are emotionally aroused, he creates a still space that works to defuse rather than fuel the tension. His is a reflective rather than reflexive response. It injects humanity and sanity into the situation. As such it enables the men to hear and respond appropriately to the question he asks. 'Let him who is without sin among you cast the first stone.'

Jesus turns the attention away from the perceived guilty party and directs it on to the accusers who up to this point consider themselves blameless. He does not abuse the woman further by focusing on her in this kangaroo court set-up. In one sense he gives the men a taste of their own medicine, putting them under the spotlight in a way they would not wish for themselves but have had no qualms about using in relation to the woman. Then again, they were the ones who raised the matter and they are, after all, in the majority. Jesus' question gets to the heart of the issue while also highlighting the bigger picture.

It's clear from the Gospels that Jesus does not accept the status quo in which few women were able to live independently and with dignity. Now, as then, inequalities in many societies place vulnerable people in difficult circumstances where they have little option but to behave in ways that those who are free of such constraints consider unacceptable. As a Palestinian friend living under occupation in the West Bank once asked, 'Why do you expect us to behave like angels when we're living in hell?'

Putting sex in its place

Jesus' question to the men cuts through their self-righteous indignation. He seems to put sexual transgressions on a par with other human failings.

In one sense he puts sex back in its place. Now, as then, we are overly preoccupied with what we consider to be inappropriate sexual activity. Thousands of people may die daily through poverty, disease, conflict and all kinds of other avoidable catastrophes, yet these tragedies receive comparatively little media attention compared with the newsprint and airtime given to the sexual exploits of those in public positions who fall short of what is expected of them. I wonder if this preoccupation is because we struggle to make sense of our own sexual experience in the light of public moral codes that fail to take seriously the questions we wrestle with in private.

Splinters and planks

Jesus' question challenges the men to think about their personal trans-gressions, sexual or otherwise; to consider the plank in their own eye, rather than the splinter in that of the woman. Now, as then, we find it much easier to focus on what we think other people are doing wrong than to acknowledge, understand and address our own faults and failings. If we did the latter we would be less judgemental and more compassionate people.

Jesus' question suggests he doesn't operate a 'sin scale' in which those listening can make themselves feel better about their own transgressions because they've decided they're not as dreadful as the failings of others. Perhaps the men in this story have never committed adultery, but like any human being they will have made destructive mistakes. What the group illustrates is bully-boy behaviour disguised as concern for communal morality. That, too, is a dynamic I recognize at work in Britain today.

Care or condemnation?

When Jesus challenges their self-righteous self-perceptions, the men to their credit get the point and back off. The woman and Jesus remain. She is, it seems, so paralysed by the trauma of this experience, perhaps hiding her face in her arms, that she does not notice the men have gone until Jesus draws her attention to the fact.

'Woman, where are they? Has no one condemned you?'

'No one, Lord.'

'Neither do I condemn you; go, and do not sin again.'

It's extraordinary, given the amount of condemnation that often accom-panies present-day conversations around sexual ethics, that, in the clear-cut instance of a woman caught having adulterous sex, Jesus does not condemn her. He tells her to go and not sin again. We assume, sex-preoccupied as we seem to be, that by 'sin' he means the adulterous sex. Mindful of his response to the men, it could be that he is telling her not to return to a situation that diminishes her humanity and colludes with the inequalities and injustices of her society. Either way, he wants her to be able to stand tall and not to be caught up in the use and abuse of others.

It has taken me many years to realize how critical it is in relation to sexual ethics to understand the context in which we wrestle with what is or is not appropriate, precisely because it may not be sex that is the issue but the inadequate understanding we have about what it is to be human.

Sex and love

I mentioned at the beginning of this chapter that the critical issue for me about any human relationship is whether or not mutual love is present in it. Personally, I can't imagine making love to someone in the absence of love. On the surface that seems a clear-cut statement, but you won't be surprised to read on and discover I think the issue is more complicated than my comment suggests. And, of course, mine is only one view among many. For other people, love doesn't have to be part of the sexual equation. They see 'having sex' as simply fulfilling a basic biological need and prefer it not to be 'complicated' by any connection beyond the sexual encounter, although they expect sexual attraction to be present. Some of the teenagers who talk with me today speak of having a 'fuck buddy'. The distasteful term and the casual nature of sex in this context disturb me. In some instances it's clear from what they say that exploitation and peer pressure are part of the equation, or they're unconsciously reacting to troubling experiences elsewhere in their lives. In other cases the young people sit easily with choosing casual encounters. For some people a monogamous lifelong relationship suits who they are, their sexual biology and personal beliefs. Yet others take on board the expectations they inherit about marriage and children but struggle to contain within that framework a sexual drive not geared for monogamy or personal experiences that make such a lifestyle difficult to maintain. Still others find life experiences as they grow older challenge the love and commitment with which they entered marriage and, wrestling with complex circumstances, they find no simple answers. For some relationships sex is not a central or essential aspect of the love shared. For other couples the sexual dynamics impact significantly for good or ill upon how they are together.

Thinking about these different approaches prompts me to ask what exactly love is. What is going on when we conclude that we love another person, and what part, if at all, does sexual intimacy play in that experience? We assume we know what we're talking about when we speak of love, but the diversity of human experience coming under that umbrella, and the difficulty we have in maintaining loving relationships, might suggest far more confusion around the subject than is generally admitted. I'll consider this more in the next chapter.

The absence of exploitation

I guess in terms of the relationship between love and sex my own basic principle is that sexual expression should not be exploitative. This is an important point because some who claim to act out of love are in fact exploiting the one they claim to love. For example, some will profess dishonestly to love a person when in reality they are simply using them. Think, too, of paedophiles who say they love the child they are abusing.

At the very least I think it is important that those engaging in sexual encounters relate as persons concerned for the well-being of each other, that sex is consensual, mutual and life-enhancing. My focus in this chapter is on ordinary people who want to get things right in this area but who sometimes struggle and fail to do so. I will not address the issues of exploitative, abusive, non-consensual sex, which are major subjects in themselves and go beyond the scope of this book, except to say that if we focus on dysfunctional sexual activity and fail to under-stand the wider factors that cause or contribute to it we are missing the point entirely and condemning millions more people to sexual harm. I might well work with the survivors of sexual violence, but if nothing is being done to challenge the cultural and religious beliefs that create the environment in which such abuse can go unchallenged, I'm only ever going to be tackling symptoms and never the cause of the problem.

My one true love?

I grew up believing that some day my prince would come! I might kiss a few frogs along the way to finding 'the One', but when we met all would become clear and we'd metaphorically ride off into the sunset to live happily ever after in wedded bliss. That's how love works, or so I thought.

Listening and learning from adults of all ages over the years who have confided in me about their relationships and the struggles that arise within those, and reflecting on my own complicated experience, suggests I might have been a tad naive in my expectations! So, after the questions ending this chapter, I'll turn to some of the issues that seem to be stumbling blocks.

Questions

1 When you were growing up what did you learn from key people in your life about love, sex and human relationships?
2 What has personal experience taught you?
3 Does your personal experience match up to the values promoted in the public domain regarding sex and love?

14

Where is love?

———————•◦•———————

Back in the Middle Ages confessional manuals of the time reveal that priests were 'expected to cross-examine penitents in a forensic manner, especially where adultery, incest and masturbation were suspected'.[1] According to John Cornwell, 'masturbation, the single greatest obsession of the confessional manuals, was judged a more serious sin than the abduction and rape of a virgin or straightforward adultery with a married woman'.[2] The reason for this was that sperm were believed to contain homunculi (completely formed little men) and therefore to waste this seed was tantamount to murder. Women were simply some kind of glorified grow bag in which the man planted the seed of fully formed but miniscule human beings!

Thankfully times and understanding have changed considerably since the Middle Ages, but this hasn't removed the need for each of us to understand the nature of our sexual drive and how to live with this powerful biological force in the context of loving relationships and healthy societies. There are plenty of books and internet sites exploring the subject in depth and it is not my intention to replicate their work. I want instead to highlight what may seem obvious facts but which I'm aware have been common stumbling blocks for many of us.

Sexual attraction is not love

There are many forms of asexual love, such as that between close friends or siblings, or between parents and children, or the sacrificial giving of a person for someone they may or may not know. The sexual drive we develop as we grow up is not something over which we have any control. Put simply it is shaped by our genetic make-up and developing biology. External factors may have some influence on this development but essentially it's something that happens regardless of what we do or don't think about it. Why, when and how we channel it is not purely biological. The life experiences and relationships that shape our inner emotional landscape and responses play a part in our attitude towards and expression of this drive. Sexual chemistry can be sparked simply by what another person looks like. It can be triggered by our imagination. It can be activated as we get to know a person better, or it may come into play the first moment we see someone.

People talk about 'love at first sight', but it's not love, it's sexual attraction and that is shaped as much by our past personal story as by the person triggering the response in the present moment. In other words, what we feel has as much, if not more, to do with who we are as who the other person is. When people get into sexual difficulties and try to understand the root causes, they often discover they have been trying unconsciously to resolve the pain of some past key relationship, or to find something that's missing in their present life. These unconscious influences may all be part of the experience we describe as 'love'. That's why I think we need to be careful about our use of the term.

The one and only?

Being in a long-term committed relationship does not switch off our capacity to be sexually attracted to other people. This capacity is neither right nor wrong. It just is. It's what we do with it that matters, and that depends upon a whole range of factors. Neither is there just one person in the world with whom we could create a long-term, loving and fulfilling relationship. The fact that we can be sexually attracted to more than one person and that there is more than one person in the world with whom we could develop a loving intimate relationship becomes problematic when love and sex are expected to come together exclusively with just one person for a lifetime. Few people have not had to wrestle with the tension this sometimes provokes in our own psyches as well as our relationships with others.

A level playing field?

To complicate matters further, we don't all have the same degree of sexual drive. In some people it is fairly latent. In others, it might be described as rampant. Some people of both sexes feel dominated by their sexual drive. They struggle to control it rather than it controlling them. This can be problematic for couples where one has a strong sexual drive and the other doesn't. Sexual fidelity will be biologically easier for some people than for others. It's also true that at different times in our lives sexual drive may be affected, as when children come on the scene, or work pressures stress us out, or illness impacts upon us. Couples can accommodate transient differing rhythms in their relationships, but long-term unfulfilled sexual energy in a partnership can be painful and problematic.

In the light of this it strikes me as strange that we make sexual fidelity the be all and end all of a good marriage. This aspect of our human biology takes precedence over such things as compassion, friendship and the kind of love that is not about sex. In reality, whatever is said publicly some couples don't see sexual infidelity as the end of their marriage. As a priest I met couples who held up sexual fidelity as the ideal but when either or both of them had been unable to maintain that the infidelity was not the end of their relationship because their love was about so much more than sex. As a nurse I met devoted couples where long-term debilitating illness had made sexual intimacy impossible for one partner. In some cases the healthy partner had developed another meaningful relationship in which sex played a part, alongside their continuing love and care for their sick spouse. One man told me that such a relationship enabled him to nurse his wife at home for many years right up until she died there.

Decades ago a woman told me that as a result of major sexual abuse in her childhood she had reached a point in her marriage when she no longer felt able to be sexually active. She knew she could not address the past cause of the problem – it was too painful – but she recognized this was profoundly difficult for her husband whose sexual drive remained as it had always been. They loved one another so neither considered divorce to be an option, but the woman had said that if any of his friendships with other women were to develop sexually, she would understand that. In sharp contrast is the experience of another woman with a similar past history who, through her choice, no longer shared a sexual relationship with her husband. When he ended up kissing another woman, she 'threw the book at him' and wanted to divorce him. I'm conscious that love was present between the first couple in a way it was absent between the second, but the woman's response in the latter will be regarded by many as right because that's what we expect.

These things are not easy, but I think a significant number of people wrestle with them, and they are not people who deliberately set out to hurt others or who are callous and unfeeling. They are simply struggling to deal with situations they never expected to face, and their humanity may be pulled apart by the differing human drives, needs, commitments and responsibilities they're trying to cope with.

Women and men are different, but . . .

Much has been written in recent years either challenging perceived differences in male and female sexuality or confirming significant differences in their sexual biology. In *Men are from Mars, Women are from Venus*,[3] John Gray suggests that women are like waves, emotionally peaking then sinking into troughs before rising to peak again, and men are like rubber bands alternately coming close and then stretching away from the beloved. I can see men and women who fit these images but I'm conscious that whenever we say 'this is how it is for women', or 'this is how it is for men', we have to acknowledge that this is not how it is for all men or all women. Male and female experience covers a spectrum and people do not fit into neat boxes. We need to get beyond the stereotypes and see each person for who he or she is as an individual.

Marriage is a human construct

Marriage has been defined by the Church as a gift from God. In reality marriage is a human construct. My friend Rabbi James Baaden has written:

> [T]he 'Old Testament', whether legalistic or not, says nothing about marriage or weddings. There are no words in Biblical Hebrew for 'marriage', 'to marry', 'wedding', etc. No weddings as such are described. Instead, men simply 'take' (or sometimes 'lift', 'pick up') women – often more than one (consider the example of Jacob – or Abraham). Accordingly, a man was also able to 'dismiss' or 'send away' a woman. This is what we encounter at least in the Pentateuch. To my mind it sounds rather far away from what we call marriage.[4]

In the Hebrew Scriptures we find polygamy as the norm. In the Gospels Jesus is critical of the man's ability simply to dismiss his wife, and the comments he makes about marriage are about rectifying this particular injustice. In the early years of the Church celibacy was considered the ideal. Before the sixteenth and seventeenth centuries, when love as a motivation for marriage began to increase in popularity, marriage was essentially a property contract in which the property of the father, namely his daughter, was given to the new husband. Canon law in the Middle Ages upheld individual choice in relation to marriage: in the Church there was unease about forced marriages. Consent was important, if not love. Slaves or serfs couldn't be compelled to marry and a person could marry in defiance of family wishes. Around the time love was becoming more central to marriage, the legal aspect of the marriage contract ceased to be conducted at home and it became a legal requirement to have a priest present at the union, now officiated over in the church. In our own day more and more wedding ceremonies are happening outside the churches.

The staff of *Psychology Today*, in the article, 'Marriage, a history', published on 1 May 2005, sum up the situation very succinctly:

Through most of Western civilization, marriage has been more a matter of money, power and survival than of delicate sentiments. In medieval Europe, everyone from the lord of the manor to the village locals had a say in deciding who should wed. Love was considered an absurdly flimsy reason for a match. Even during the Enlightenment and Victorian eras, adultery and friendship were often more passionate than marriage. These days, we marry for love – and are rewarded with a blistering divorce rate.[5]

The reasons for our present divorce rate are varied but it's worth noting the impact of increased lifespan. We live considerably longer than our ancestors. Today there are more so-called 'silver splitters' than ever before. The experience of these often long-married couples, divorcing after the age of 60, suggests that there is a change in attitudes towards marriage. Veteran Labour politician Roy Hattersley, for example, was 80 when he and his wife of 57 years, Molly, divorced.

What is clear is that marriage has been a changing feature of human life and for much of its history had nothing to do with love. We continue today to try and work out the nature of loving relationships, sexual expression and its place within human experience, and the best environment in which to raise children. This can be really difficult but it can also be creative. Rabbi James Baaden sees the notable gap in the Hebrew Bible concerning marriage as something positive because it makes room for conversation about what relationships might look like in any given time and context. Nothing is set in stone.

All we need is each other?

No one person can ever fulfil all my needs, nor can I ever fulfil all those of another person, however much we love one another. I cycle with friends, or do outdoor adventure activities with my son, because Chris isn't sporty like me. He discusses academic philosophy with his friends because that's his passion, not mine. I work with colleagues in relation to conflict transformation, which isn't his interest. He needs lots of time on his own because that feeds his spirit in a way I can't. This recognition of one person not being able to fulfil all our needs generally doesn't extend to our sexual needs. Of course we express love and affection physically in a range of relationships, kissing and hugging certain people when we meet, or offering physical touches of comfort to people with whom we share care and friendship, like holding a person's hand or putting an arm round their shoulder. But for most people sexual desire for a person other than one's partner must be left at the door, acknowledged as present, maybe, but not given admittance because that way lies death and destruction. The words of the Marriage Service are clear: we must 'forsake all others'. There is much wisdom in these words.

Commitment to working with complexity

I've already noted that attraction to another person may say far more about personal past experience and present challenges than who that person is. I've acknowledged, too, that these things unconsciously influence what we define as 'love'. Couples know that part of developing a long-term relationship is about getting to know and love who the other person really is, warts and all, rather than holding on to what we need and want them to be. When Chris and I were preparing to get married we both thought of a book that captured the essence of our life before we met one another. I chose Enid Blyton's *Famous Five* and Chris picked Charles Dickens' *Bleak House*. The choices illustrate well the challenge we had to weave these two very different stories into the new narrative of our life together: a simple example being my desire for adventure (ginger beer not essential!) conflicting with his need for a quiet contented life.

Loving another person isn't always feeling good about them. Sometimes it's tough as we wrestle with each other's sharp edges and wounded selves, and learn to work with our own. The commitment of the relationship to be there for one another no matter what is what provides the safety to explore who we are in ways we can't do with anyone else. At least that's how we feel when we start out. Couples coming to speak to me about getting married often say the person they love is someone with whom they can share anything. Further down the line of being married, when the more challenging aspects of any long-term loving relationship kick in, those same people no longer feel able to be open. At one level this is understandable. They don't want to hurt the other person with the less edifying or unhappy thoughts and feelings they have, or they fear rejection. They worry these difficult reactions are an indication of the relationship failing, rather than recognizing them as part and parcel of the work any relationship, however deep, demands in complex contexts. Because they no longer feel able to be honest, pressure builds up, rather like steam in a pressure cooker, adding to the difficulties. If relationships develop elsewhere, trust is seen to have been broken. Perhaps things might be different if there was greater recognition of human complexity, and therefore honesty was less threatening.

Relationships change and develop, positively and negatively, as people and circumstances change and develop. Sometimes the shared life feels great and sometimes it is hard graft, and the grass may look greener elsewhere. The marriage commitment is about being there for each other whatever happens, 'for better, for worse, for richer, for poorer, in sickness and in health, to love and to cherish, till death us do part', as it says in the Marriage Service. Sometimes today, it seems, the moment problems arise, particularly those of a sexual nature, one or other partner immediately leaves the relationship. Is that to do with any sexual infidelity, or a lack of understanding about human beings and the nature of long-term committed and loving relationships?

Working with reality

If forsaking all others is wise, it is also difficult as people wrestle with the complexities of sexual drive, what love is or isn't, the impact of the past on the present, and who they are becoming in all of this. There is a much greater need for compassion in this area of human experience. None of us are perfect. We will get things wrong in all kinds of different ways, some of them to do with sexual expression, some not. Caring sensitivity not stark censure is what's needed. As the writer Frances Partridge put it, 'I hate the stupid geometrical figures by which people try to understand the emotions of others, imposing hard straight lines – or "sides" as they call them, onto tender curvaceous human beings who have none.'[6]

Honesty and trust

Partridge was part of an influential group of artists, philosophers, writers and intellectuals in the first half of the twentieth century. They came to be known as the Bloomsbury Group and deeply influenced literature, aesthetics, economics and modern attitudes to the role of women, pacifism and sexuality. Familiar names among their number include Leonard and Virginia Woolf, Vanessa and Clive Bell, Lytton Strachey, Duncan Grant, Dora Carrington and E. M. Forster. They were highly influenced by George E. Moore, Professor of Philosophy at Cambridge, for whom seeking knowledge, the creation and enjoyment of aesthetic experience and love were key motivations for life.

Some of them advocated and practised polyamory, having multiple consensual romantic partners, heterosexual and homosexual. This was shocking in Edwardian England and their sexual exploits brought them very negative and mocking attention in the press. What I find compelling about their sexual expression is the honesty of it, however complicated and difficult their relationships sometimes were. They recognized the complexity of human loving relationships and sexuality, and worked to live with it, not pretend it didn't exist.

Frances Partridge challenged the often expressed idea that the Bloomsbury Group was 'unconventional'. It 'suggests deliberate flouting of rules;
it was rather that they were quite uninterested in conventions, but
passionately in ideas'.[7] She had little time herself for social conventions,
which 'have always seemed to me a means of avoiding thinking out
one's own values, and clinging blindly to the security of being like other
people'.[8] When Frances fell in love with Ralph Partridge he was already
married to Dora Carrington. Carrington was deeply in love with Lytton
Strachey, who was gay. They had a devoted friendship and lived together.
Both had lovers. After the initial impact and upheaval of Frances' and
Ralph's relationship the four were the closest friends. An abiding reflection of Frances regarding the Bloomsbury Group is that, whatever the
emotional traumas, honesty and friendship prevailed among them.

The experience of the Bloomsbury Group seems to suggest that
sexual fidelity need not be the defining feature of a good marriage. Trust,
kindness, commitment and compassion are essential. Love is not about
having exclusive rights over the sexual expression of another human
being. Frances and her close circle of friends maintained trust because
they were able to be honest about their sexuality, the complexities
of loving and the realities of being human. This did not necessarily
make for an easy life. There was certainly much pain in the emotional
lives of some members of the circle, although factors other than
personal relationships played a part in that. Their views also put them
at odds with wider society. Whatever advances we have made since
then, we still remain censorious and judgemental, thereby making it
difficult for people to be honest in their key relationships. When these
become complicated the lack of honesty may lead to broken trust and
profound pain.

I have no doubt that profound love may arise between two people
who are also married to partners they love. Love doesn't always conform
to our expectations, but any relationship of any value takes time and
effort to sustain and develop. This point should give us much pause for
thought. Loving relationships are dynamic. When they are not given
space and enabled to expand and be what they have it in them to be,
the love, and one or both of the lovers, end up getting crucified. What
was life-giving becomes death-dealing. This can happen in both con-
ventional and unconventional relationships where what exists is concealed
and confined. Love of any kind deserves better than that.

Like so many other areas of human experience, I suspect there are
no easy or uniform answers to these issues. Most of us are on journeys
of discovery for which, for the most part, we are ill-prepared. Perhaps
if we were a little more aware about the nature of human relationships
we would deal more compassionately with others and ourselves.

For me, any kind of lukewarm attitude or fearful sitting on the fence is an affront to love. Compassion and sensitivity are crucial, but so is passion. Life is to be lived to the full, not to be avoided for fear of failure or rejection or finding ourselves sometimes out of our depth. The intensity of knowing another and oneself deeply is captured for me in David Whyte's poem, 'Self Portrait':

> ### Self portrait
> It doesn't interest me if there is one God
> or many gods.
> I want to know if you belong or feel
> abandoned.
> If you know despair or can see it in others.
> I want to know
> if you are prepared to live in the world
> with its harsh need
> to change you. If you can look back
> with firm eyes
> saying this is where I stand. I want to know
> if you know
> how to melt into that fierce heat of living
> falling toward
> the center of your longing. I want to know
> if you are willing
> to live, day by day, with the consequence of love
> and the bitter
> unwanted passion of your sure defeat.
>
> I have heard, in *that* fierce embrace, even
> the gods speak of God.[9]

Such passion needs containment if it is to enhance rather than destroy our lives through the power it releases. In each of the areas I've explored so far, power plays a part. In the next section I'll reflect on this potent aspect of being human.

Questions

1 What would help you to live with the complexities of love and sexual expression?
2 What are the questions you have around these experiences?
3 Where might you be able to address these issues safely if you wanted or needed to do this?

Part 7

POWER

15

How are the mighty fallen

The isle of Iona off the west coast of Scotland is called a 'thin place': for people of faith it's where the things of God feel close. In AD 563 St Columba arrived by boat from Ireland and founded the island's first monastery. Fast forward to 1938, when the Revd George McCleod set up the Iona Community. He was working as a parish minister in Govan, a greatly deprived district in Glasgow. He came to the island with young parishioners and men training for priesthood, with the purpose of rebuilding the abbey. The community he established is ecumenical. While its heart might be said to beat on Iona, Community members are dispersed across the world, sharing a rule of life and a commitment to social justice and radical theology. Those who work on the island lead the contemporary and contemplative worshipping life of the Community, and run workshops on all kinds of subjects.

Sanctity and struggle

Today, Iona is somewhere I feel free. The poet Kenneth C. Steven captures the experience for me in one of his Iona poems:

Resolution
And suddenly the sun broke through the sky
And I was home, a broad Atlantic
Stumbled over rocks and creamed in rage
A tug of storm hung low across the shores
Water colour blue and broken green.

How did I lose my way or once believe
That there were riches bigger than this simplicity
Or that any other tide could speak, or heal
The wounds of searching deeper cut than pain
Where here I stood by heaven hearing God?[1]

The temptation to overstate the sense of 'heaven on earth' I always feel when I go to Iona is great, but even as I give in to it I am conscious of how that sense of the sacred is created as much by the very human wrestling with complexity that is part of the Community's life and work, as by the natural beauty of the place and the spiritual history that infuses its very stones.

Gender politics

Around the time the first women in the Church of England, including me, were ordained as priests I co-led a week-long workshop on the island on the subject of gender issues. The people who book a week in the Abbey do not always come because they are interested in the programme for that time, but because a room is free or they must take their holiday then, so our group gathered with very mixed agendas. During one session when we were discussing power and authority, one of the men said, 'When I go on holiday, I never leave a woman in charge of the factory. If I did they'd have their knickers off in no time.' His words were greeted by the shocked sound of dropping jaws hitting the floor. One woman left the room in tears and others began to respond vocally, leaving the man in no doubt how deeply offensive they found his sentiments. One or two had been the victims of sexual abuse. Others had been banging their heads on the glass ceiling of their various working environments seeking to break into all-male leadership domains. The man was genuinely taken aback by the impact of his remarks. It had not occurred to him that he was saying anything unusually controversial. As is the potential of conversations that arise out of painful encounters, the discussion that followed ultimately became a source of breakthrough for a number of the people involved, including the man who'd spoken and the woman who'd left the room in deep distress at his words.

Ignoring the uncomfortable obvious?

When I returned home I mentioned the man's comment in my Sunday sermon. How can it be, I asked the congregation, that a person who has been a member of the Church for over 40 years can make such a comment and see no problem with the sexism and misogyny expressed? There was shock among some of my listeners but not, as became clear after the service, at the man's prejudice. What was unacceptable for some members of the congregation was that I had said the word 'knickers' in the pulpit. Such was the strength of feeling about the matter that a special meeting was called. My heart sank when an elderly woman I didn't yet know, but assumed to be conservative, got up to speak first. 'I can't understand what all the fuss is about,' she said. 'We should be focusing on the sexism Ruth's story illustrates and not her repetition of the word "knickers" in the pulpit. That's a complete red herring.' How I loved Laure from that moment on!

This anecdote captures for me much of what will come up in this chapter. I'll be looking at the relationship between power and language, and how that changes in different contexts. I'll suggest that few if any of us can use power without at some point abusing it, and explore why I think this is the case.

Power and language

In our society power and language are closely connected. This link is illustrated in the two creation myths of the Judeo-Christian tradition in which Western civilization is rooted. In the first story of creation at the beginning of Genesis, God speaks creation into existence from the formless void. His words bring order. They break into the 'silence', rather like the Big Bang of present-day cosmology. Whether we can talk about silence being broken with words or bangs of any volume when there are no ears present to hear is another matter, but it is no accident that in this particular creation story it is language that brings all things into being – perhaps because humankind doesn't sit easily with silence. It unnerves many of us.

Silence is golden?

In *A Book of Silence*, which charts her love affair with silence, Sara Maitland speaks about how in Western society many of us see silence as 'an absence and a dangerous absence at that'.[2] For me, silence is the exact opposite: it is the presence of all things and in deep silences I have no sense of aloneness but of complete 'at one-ness' in the present moment, to the extent that I lose all sense of me and of time until I 'come back to myself' and realize how much time has passed. The opposite is true for Maitland's friend Janet. She speaks of silence as oppression, arguing that it is 'the word' which is the beginning of freedom. Language liberates. 'All silence is waiting to be broken,' she says.[3]

Language and power

According to the creation myths of Genesis, power comes with language. In the second story this empowerment is captured in God's invitation to Adam, the 'earth being', to name what God has created. This gives Adam power over what he names. If power comes with language, so too does the capacity to abuse that power. To dominate is to exercise power inappropriately over something or someone else. The language of abusive power is adversarial and aggressive in patriarchal societies. It often reflects testosterone-fuelled instincts that are about gaining, marking and protecting territory and, for some, attracting fertile females to impregnate and carry on the line. However civilized we think we are as a society these instincts are clear for all to see in any institution or community, particularly, but not exclusively, those that rely heavily on competitive edge for success.

Power and pride

The descendants of Adam didn't take long to abuse the power God had given them. In the story of the Great Flood we read how God becomes so put out about the behaviour of humankind he wipes them off the face of the earth, save for Noah and his family. (The God of these stories is clearly a human creation amplifying characteristics reflecting our behaviour rather than anything remotely divine.) After the flood the surviving descendants of Noah forget quickly what happens when men get 'above themselves'. They develop great skills and are so proud of their abilities they decide to build a tower reaching to heaven, thus elevating themselves to God-like status. God sees what they are doing and foils their plan by confusing their language so that they no longer all speak in the same tongue. The story of the Tower of Babel illustrates how, when we think we can be as God in heaven, pride and our misplaced sense of power usually come before a fall, when our way of being is broken up and something new has to emerge that is about more than power and the control of others.

Language and behaviour

Language is not just words. It reflects and shapes our attitudes and actions. Alistair, the friend and colleague I've mentioned in earlier chapters, speaks about how violent language and swearing were the norm for him and his paramilitary peers. When, during his time in the Maze prison, he began to move away from seeing violence as a solution to the problems and gradually became more involved in peace-building, he consciously decided to stop swearing. For him there was a strong connection between violent language and violent action.

The Jesus of Matthew's Gospel says, 'Listen and understand: it is not what goes into the mouth that defiles a person, but it is what comes out of the mouth that defiles' (Matt. 15.10–11). In our language we see expressed the heights of human poetry and profundity and the harsh prejudice and profanity of which we are equally capable. The way we use language often makes explicit the areas of our understanding that are out of balance. Think, for example, about the portrayal of women in language.

Language and liberty

In the Bible only a minority of women are deemed significant enough to name compared to the number of named men. Biblical storytelling is, for the most part, concerned with the male line and the stories of men. In the English language women were often subsumed into male terms like 'mankind' and 'all men'. Language reflected the invisibility of women in society and the secondary place they held. It helped to keep them invisible. Only in my lifetime has significant attention been brought to this absence and the way it reflects attitudes towards, and actions against, the liberty and equality of women.

Despite its limitations, the sophistication of human language and the capacity it gives us for self-reflection sets us apart from other species. It's how we gain knowledge, and knowledge is power. When our car broke down as we arrived at a holiday destination and we took it to the local garage we were at the mercy of the mechanics since their expertise was not ours. We knew enough to determine the clutch had packed up, but all the other things we were told needed repair when the car was looked at we had to take on trust. With greater knowledge – in this case about motor mechanics – we would have known what questions to ask or been able to recognize if we were being 'taken for a ride'.

Language and communication

It seems obvious to state that language is the means by which we acquire knowledge, but things are more complicated than that. In Chapter 3 I spoke about Iain McGilchrist's extraordinary book *The Master and His Emissary*. Iain puts forward evidence from such fields of investigation as the fossil record, anthropology and neuroscience to show that before we had language we had music, and that language is not necessary for communication or for thinking. He writes:

> We may find it initially hard to accept the primacy of music, since we are trapped inside a culture that is so language-determined and language dependent that we cannot imagine it being any other way ... What we are not conscious of, and need for most purposes to remain unconscious of, is that the majority of the messages we communicate are not in words at all.[4]

He goes on to say:

> It is estimated that even now over 90 per cent of communication between humans is by non-verbal means ... In fact, even without the anthropological evidence, we might well be doubtful that language was needed for communication, if for no other reason than that language, unlike more intuitive, musical, forms of communication, is the perfect medium for concealing rather than revealing meaning.[5]

McGilchrist highlights the link between language and tool-making, which is associated with the development of right-hand skill. The location of grasp in the left hemisphere of the brain is close to that of speech, bringing a connection between language and manipulation. The link comes out in what we say when we don't understand something. We talk about 'not being able to grasp it' or 'not being able to put our finger on it'. McGilchrist writes:

> The idea of 'grasping' implies seizing a thing for ourselves, for use, for wrestling it away from its context, holding it fast, focussing on it. The grasp we have, our understanding in this sense, is the expression of our will, and it is the means to power. It is what enables us to 'manipulate' – literally to take a handful of whatever we need – and thereby to dominate the world around us.[6]

Prioritizing verbal language, with its relationship to power and manipulation, rather than putting it in its proper place as one among a number of ways in which human beings engage with and understand reality and communicate, creates an imbalance which means that we are already susceptible to abusing the power we have and understanding inadequately our place in the world. It makes us more prone to prioritize things that can be pinned down factually than to give proper weight to the non-verbal imaginative languages of art, music, physical theatre and dance.

'I am that I am'

In biblical mythology to know the name of someone is to have power over them, which is why, when Moses asks the name of God, God replies, 'I am that I am', in other words, mind your own business! For all the inadequate, all-too-human pictures of God in the books of the Bible, Judeo–Christian tradition knows that what we symbolize by the word 'God' transcends time and space and cannot be known and expressed in the same way we articulate physical realities that are limited by time and space. It is a common human error either to believe that we can pin down God or to put other people on a pedestal giving them God-like status they cannot embody.

One year when I was speaking with a colleague at the Edinburgh International Book Festival, Richard Dawkins, biologist and outspoken atheist, came into the Authors' Tent surrounded by a small group of people who seemed attentive to his every need. I pointed him out to my agnostic colleague, who watched for a few minutes and then said, 'It's strange how someone who doesn't believe in God seems to enjoy being treated like one!' When we attribute God-like status to someone else – 'He's my hero', 'She's a saint' – that person may have particular human qualities we lack, but putting someone on a pedestal can be a way of abdicating personal responsibility for the life of our community. Behind the words, 'She's so wonderful. I couldn't possibly do what she does', is a sense of relief that we are too 'inadequate' to do what needs to be done.

Abdicating power

For many of us the failure to utilize responsibly the degree of power we have often results either from the misguided belief that we are powerless or because we do not want the responsibility that comes with power. We may not want to carry the can if things go wrong on our watch, or we may have other things we'd prefer to be doing. There's a tension here between wanting to be in control of our own destiny and being fearful of using the power we have because of the responsibility that comes with it. When human beings get an inflated sense of their own importance or power, the potential for the abuse of power is great.

Much of the Hebrew Scriptures might be seen as man's (I use the term deliberately) struggle with power. Some are heroes who rise and then fall, as in the story of David, the simple shepherd boy who saves his people, is made their king and then becomes corrupt. Others are consistently complex characters. Take Moses, who at different times embodies humanity and inhumanity, clear vision and blind arrogance. He can be seen as both powerful and powerless, sometimes at one and the same time, depending on your perspective. In moments when his people look to him as the one who knows what to do, he is clueless about the way forward. Inarticulate Moses, feeling wholly inadequate for the task, liberates his people from slavery in Egypt and is seen as a great leader . . . just so long as he provides what his people need.

Earlier in this book I spoke of the confrontation between my son, Tian, and myself when I was trying unsuccessfully to get him ready for school one morning. I was the one with the power. I was the parent. Yet, in the face of my son's behaviour I reached a point of feeling powerless. His non-cooperation was powerful in its effect upon me. I lost the plot and reacted with rage. In that moment Tian was the potential victim, powerless against my fury. Power and powerless can sometimes be one and the same thing, and it's also worth noting that the power I attribute to others, or they attribute to me, may only exist in our perception of one another and not in what each is actually feeling in that moment.

Men of power in ancient myth

It's not surprising, given how much through human history we struggle to use power appropriately, that profound stories concerning power remain ever popular. In Greek mythology there are countless examples of men or the offspring of human–divine couplings becoming heroes and leaders of their people, only to fall into the arrogance of believing themselves invincible, infallible and immortal to the detriment of themselves and all who serve or love them. Odysseus is a classic example. For ten years he achieves hero status in the Trojan War, but he develops an inflated sense of himself that leads to ten further years of disastrous journeying by sea and the loss of all his companions.

Jungian analyst Helen Luke points out that the latter ten years of Odysseus' experience 'involved confrontations with various aspects of the feminine unconscious',[7] personified by such secondary goddesses as Circe, the Sirens, Scylla and Calypso. 'It is perhaps the greatest story in western literature of a man's journey in search of his feminine soul and of the dangers he must face from the rejected feeling values of the unconscious.'[8]

Later in the story Odysseus makes another journey, inland this time, to a place where he must plant the oar he has carried with him and sacrifice to Poseidon a ram, a bull and a breeding boar, powerful symbols of male potency. It seems that the key to using our power effectively is to hold in balance, or tension, what might be described as masculine and feminine elements of our own psyches and, beyond the individual self, within wider society. These elements may alternatively be seen as differing motivations like strength and gentleness, justice and mercy, pride and humility, or passion and patience. When one dominates at the expense of the other, then we are likely to abuse our power.

We tend to think in terms of human beings having good or bad elements within them, but the same characteristic may have the potential to be either a force for good or a force for evil. What determines the outcome is the motivation for its use. Strength motivated by love may help to build up the common good, while strength motivated by hatred or greed may destroy it. Clarity of vision, as illustrated in the story of Odysseus, requires balance in the human psyche. So the voice of Truth without the voice of Love can be cruel, and the voice of Love without the voice of Truth can be sentimental. In many myths these differing voices are illustrated by male and female characters. There is clearly gender stereotyping in their portrayal but whether or not we would attribute the drives to one or other gender, the differences of being are important, as is the need to hold them within our own psyches in the right balance.

Questions

1 What does the word 'power' mean for you?
2 How is power present in your own life, and who holds it?
3 In what ways do you think society today is out of balance?

16

True power

———————

Although ancient, the story of Odysseus persists into our own time because it captures what is true in human experience in all times and places. Think for a moment of what was until recently a largely male domain, the House of Commons. It is physically set up in adversarial style with opposing parties facing each other across the chamber. Running a few feet in front and along the length of each front bench is a red strip. I've been told no MPs are allowed to step across these lines during debates. The gap between the two lines is supposedly wide enough to keep apart two men brandishing swords! Today, in the absence of swords we see instead at Prime Minister's question time the sometimes farcical spectacle of the Prime Minister and the Leader of the Opposition verbally sparring with one another. Testosterone levels are high on the floor of the House and egos are on display for all to see. This often does a great injustice to those MPs who come into politics because they see or have experienced injustice and want to challenge and change that reality.

Communities out of balance

Energy Minister Baroness Verma of Leicester said in an interview reported in *The Guardian* that the biggest barrier to women in politics was 'the way we conduct it ... I'm not a supporter of bang-on-tables and be adversarial in politics and I still think that puts a lot of women off.'[1] She noted that the hectoring behaviour expected of her and other politicians in debate is the kind of behaviour parents spend their time telling their children is unacceptable.

Adversarial debating formats find expression in sometimes unexpected settings. When the General Synod of the Church of England meets, its pattern of governance has very much the feel of parliamentary democracy. In November 2012 the General Synod voted narrowly against the appointment of women as bishops. The vote was passed by the Houses of Bishops and Clergy but failed to get the necessary two-thirds majority in the House of Laity. The result received widespread condemnation in the media. It raised questions about how representative the House of

Laity was, given that 42 out of 44 dioceses had voted in favour of the legislation before it came to General Synod. The barrage of abusive correspondence received in the aftermath of the vote left many members of General Synod feeling deeply wounded by the experience.

I was one of a group of facilitators and mediators invited to lead a day of facilitated conversations at the following July General Synod in 2013. The membership was divided into groups of 20 and we guided them through a carefully designed process that took seriously the pain and anger that were present and explored ways of going forward in the light of what had happened. What struck me profoundly was the number of members who told me how helpful they found these facilitated difficult conversations, which were the antithesis of people taking a stand against one another and focused on working effectively together with the diametrically opposed opinions represented. 'I wish we could work more often in this way,' was a repeated comment.

The focus shifted from winning or losing to determining whether the commitment existed to being a community in which diverse perspectives could be held and, if it did, how this might be lived out creatively rather than the Church being ripped apart by dissenting voices. 'Us and them' becomes 'we'. This did not mean there was no room for anger, frustration, pain and all the normal reactions that are part of creative conflict. What changed was the way in which people dealt with these. The move was away from seeking to gain power from or over the opposition to sharing power with them. This is much harder to effect than adversarial politics and the taking or losing of power that are part of that. Baroness Verma's comments seem to suggest that women tend to work more to this pattern – when they are able to do so – preferring less confrontational ways of dealing with areas of difference and difficult decision-making.

In the same paper the day after the interview with Baroness Verma, broadcaster Sandi Toksvig was reported lamenting the lack of women on quiz shows, saying that programmes like *Mock the Week* are 'dominated by men, who are prepared to be aggressive'.[2] Her comments came in the same week that a National Union of Journalists report noted that in the BBC 140 allegations of bullying made by staff against senior managers remained unresolved. Bullying is a classic symptom of an individual or system out of balance.

Claims of bullying by senior politicians have also been in the news in recent times. Bullies are unable to handle power appropriately, usually because they are insecure and inadequate in some way, and lack the people skills to work with others creatively. Where diverse voices are able to question the status quo, abuses of power are much less likely to go unchallenged, and are therefore less likely to happen in the first place. The expenses scandal showed how cut-off some MPs had become from the expectations of their constituents and from what is appropriate regardless of what was considered acceptable in the culture of Parliament.

None of these unacceptable patterns of behaviour – egotistical and childish posturing in debates, bullying, taking what you can get when it's not appropriate – are the sole preserve of MPs. Stories of politicians making unjustifiable expenses claims shared news space with accounts of benefit fraud. Alongside those people with genuine needs, for whom government benefit cuts were causing increasing hardship, there were also individuals claiming thousands of pounds' worth of benefits to which they were not entitled.

If I'm honest I know I too behave at times in the same childish, egotistical manner I hate watching on the floor of Parliament. I too need the wisdom of balancing perspectives and diverse voices to help me see the 'lie' I sometimes live. The expenses scandal is a classic example of what happens when we become disconnected from the voices that help us to understand our folly and to recognize when we are abusing the power we have sought or others have invested in us.

Brokenness and power

In Shakespeare's *The Tempest*, Prospero ends up abandoned on a desert island with his daughter Miranda, in part because he gave over much of his power as Duke of Milan to his brother Antonio, who ultimately conspired against him and had him put out of the dukedom.

Prospero is saved from insanity by his love for and devotion to his daughter Miranda, his feminine principle. Creating the tempest that wrecks their ship, he draws into his domain those responsible for his downfall. As the play unfolds we see Prospero's struggle with his desire to dominate, even destroy, those who have wronged him, alongside his wish for restoration of himself and his relationships. These two competing drives are embodied in the magical characters of Ariel and Caliban. Caliban is a monster of a creature who is kept chained up by Prospero.

I am aware of aspects of my own psyche that disturb me greatly and feel a threat to my well-being. I try but don't always succeed in keeping them in check, just as Prospero wrestles with Caliban. *The Tempest* explores one man's struggle in relation to personal demons and abusive power. In the end, for Prospero to be fully human and fully himself, he must reconcile his broken relationships, relinquish his book of magic words and storm-raising staff and give freedom to Ariel and Caliban. Caliban is not destroyed. He is recognized for what he is, not the demon that must be forever subdued but part of the nature of every person that once understood ceases to be a threat.

For us, as for Prospero, the integration of all the disparate elements of who we are, including those aspects we wish did not exist, is what leads us into a true humanity that no longer seeks the power of domination but looks only to restored relationship and in return is freed from the dominating aspects of who we are.

Purpose and power

The Tempest illustrates a connection between the desire for power and the damaged self. One might say that no one in their right mind seeks power. This suggests we might want to consider carefully those who actively seek out positions of power because they want power. Nelson Mandela and Aung San Suu Kyi are examples of two people who did not seek power, but who in working for justice emerged as leaders. Personal power was not their purpose, and purpose is key when it comes to how we use power. In *Voltaire's Bastards*, John Ralston Saul, author, essayist and President of PEN International, writes this of the relationship between power and purpose:

> The Age of Reason has turned out to be the Age of Structure; a time when, in the absence of purpose, the drive for power as a value in itself has become the principal indicator of social approval. And the winning of power has become the measure of social merit.[3]

In the Church of England people do not apply for the position of Archbishop of Canterbury, and a good job too: you wouldn't want the person who thought they were right for the job. A good appointment depends in part upon there being adequate representation of diverse perspectives in the selection process, rather than particular interest groups exerting inappropriate influence.

In ancient Greece, sortition was used in many city states, like Athens. Sortition is the selection of decision-makers by lottery from a larger pool of people. The Athenians thought this way of working was more democratic than elections and less open to the abuse of power and corruption because they used complex procedures and purpose-built allotment machines to prevent people buying their way into power. This system provided some practical political education for its citizens so that responsibility was shared. Of course, Greek society was not entirely democratic. Women had little or no voice politically, and only those who put their names forward were part of the lottery, but it seems to me the practice has something to offer in the present day, given everything I've said about power and its abuse. Our own legal system uses the process in the selection of juries.

Redefining power

Perhaps another way of limiting the capacity we all have to abuse power is to redefine it. The Hebrew Scriptures begin with the myth of God speaking creation into being and emphasizing the power of the spoken word, with all the complications this brings.

The Gospel of John in the Christian Scriptures begins poetically as follows:

> In the beginning was the Word, and the Word was with God, and the Word was God ...
>
> And the Word became flesh and lived among us, and we have seen his glory, the glory as of a father's only son, full of grace and truth. (John 1.1, 14)

John portrays Jesus as the eternal Word, not only up there with God but of one being with God, the pinnacle of power. His words seem to embody every idea of power I've been challenging in this chapter. But that is only part of the picture. The Gospel narratives also subvert human concepts of power. In key moments when men around him are shouting the odds, baying for blood or demanding some vulnerable person gets their just desserts, Jesus the Word falls silent. I wrote about this in Chapter 13 in relation to the story of the woman taken in adultery. The power of Jesus' silence is to still the voices around him so that when he speaks his words come out of the silence and work to greater effect than if he had shouted above the clamour of voices.

Later in the story, when Jesus has been brought before Pilate and his life is on the line, his words are minimal, until he finally ceases to answer any more questions. His silence throws Pilate, causing him to wonder at the man before him.

Images, like the cross and empty tomb, exert a greater power over the human imagination than many of the words that have been spoken in the name of Christianity, but some of the words remembered are of notions of power being turned upside down. Jesus is a servant king who washes his disciples' feet, causing them to look down to the realm of those brought low by the inhumanity of others, rather than looking up to heaven and arguing about who will exercise power at the right and left hand of Jesus. The Jesus of the Gospels of Matthew, Mark and Luke declares, 'many that are first will be last, and the last first'. The words confirm the song of Mary, the Magnificat, in Luke's Gospel, echoing voices from the Psalms, Isaiah and Job, in which 'he has scattered the proud in the imagination of their hearts, he has put down the mighty from their seat, and exalted those of low degree'.

Power as service

Focusing on the needs of others who are cast down changes the way in which we understand and use power. Power is for the service of others, not self-promotion and selfish gain. Structures and processes that diminish some while satisfying the greed of others are no longer acceptable. Recognizing that no one person can hold power without being corrupted by it calls for greater responsibility among all of us in addressing the issues of our day and in making sure a diversity of perspectives are represented in any group of people involved in appointing others to power. We might also take more seriously the potential of those who neither desire nor feel equipped to exercise power and question the appropriateness of those who actively seek it.

Perhaps the distinguishing feature between people like Jesus, Nelson Mandela and Aung San Suu Kyi is that they do not need external positions of power. They have inner authority, born from a profound engagement with humanity in all its many shades. Jacques Maritain, Catholic philosopher and prominent drafter of the Universal Declaration of Human Rights, distinguishes between power and authority in this way:

> Authority and power are two different things: power is the force by means of which you can oblige others to obey you. Authority is the right to direct and command, to be listened to or obeyed by others. Authority requests power. Power without authority is tyranny.[4]

If we recognize that aspirations to power often arise in the absence of inner authority and integrity of being, and we recognize that abuses of power by the supposedly powerful and the seemingly powerless are abuses of which we are all capable, then in accepting this reality we can offer still spaces amid the clamorous words of confusion and conflict increasingly dominating today's world. In that silence perhaps a new sense of purpose may come to shape our perceptions and practice, and perpetuate the kind of power that seeks to wash feet not steal crowns of undeserved glory.

Knowing when to speak and when to keep silent is an important skill. The same is true of knowing what should remain in the private domain and what needs to be part of public discourse for human well-being – the focus of the final chapters in this book.

Questions

1 How do you use your own power?
2 Do you challenge the misuse of power wherever you see it?
3 What could you do to make sure power is used wisely?

Part 8

PRIVACY

17

Justice or just us?

———·◆·———

When I was eight years old my big brother told me about 'a short cut from school that's much more fun than going our usual way'. I was eager to try it. It involved diverting down a dead-end road that culminated in a six-foot wall separating the street from the hospital beyond. We scaled the wall, jumped down the other side and ran along a gap between a prefab day room and a row of shrubs, crouching low to avoid being seen by the old people lined around the day-room walls. At the other end of the building was another wall to climb. The next bit was the most dangerous. We dropped from the wall into a rose bed which offered no cover. It was visible to anyone looking out from the hospital windows. Once through that we were shielded again by a row of evergreen trees running alongside the staff tennis courts to the main gate where we reconnected with what remained of our usual route.

One day a gardener caught me in the rose garden and demanded to know what I was doing. 'I'm working on a school nature project,' I blurted out before losing my cool and running hell for leather for the gate.

Some weeks and several more exciting hospital dashes later, Mr Pledger, our lovely head teacher, came into my classroom. Something very serious had come to light, he said. A number of pupils from our school had been trespassing in the gardens of St Peter's Hospital and disturbing the patients. He wanted to know if anyone in this class had been running through the hospital grounds. He stopped talking and waited. My heart was racing and my face flushed with guilt and shame, but I kept quiet. After a few moments he said that if any of us had been involved it would be better to admit it now than to say nothing, which was dishonest and a bad thing. Was anyone in the class guilty of this crime? I sweated only a few moments more before putting up my hand. I was, after all, my parents' child and a devout churchgoer; how could I not confess my guilt?

'Did you do this often?' asked Mr Pledger.

'No, only once,' I lied. There's only so much truth 'my parents' child and devout churchgoer' could manage!

Come-uppance

Mr Pledger, of course, knew I was part of the wayward gang. A sneaky fellow culprit called Richard Johnson had grassed on me after he'd been questioned by the Head! It turned out that 15 boys and I had enjoyed the 'assault course' through the hospital. At break and lunchtime on that fateful day the 15 lads were lined up facing the playground wall. I'm not sure if I was spared this humiliation and punishment because I owned up to the crime, if not the number of times I'd committed it, or because I was a girl, or because I was the only girl. A special assembly was called at the end of the day. The boys were again all made to line up at the front. I kept as low a profile as possible among my cross-legged classmates near the back of the hall as Mr Pledger talked about what had happened, his disappointment at the behaviour of the 'fifteen boys and one girl' involved, and his expectation that none of the pupils would ever do such a thing again.

I might have remained anonymous at this point were it not for the fact that it was Friday and on Fridays I left school five minutes early to scooter to my piano lesson two miles away. Thus it was that, as Mr Pledger spoke, my form teacher came down between the lines of us, parting the waves of children like Moses in the Red Sea, to seize me by the shoulder and haul me out for my music lesson, leaving no one in any doubt that I was the one girl.

I was terrified of my parents being told. For days I waited for the trouble I was sure was imminent. It didn't come. I don't know how much later I learnt from our beloved vicar that he had told my parents and in the telling had found it so amusing they decided the exposure of what I'd done had been punishment enough and let the matter lie. With his assurances about this I was finally able to let go of the whole episode and move on, although I never did cope well with failure after that. My brother was mortified to hear how his little sister had fainted with the shock of being given a demerit for not handing in her biology homework in the second year of secondary school. What kind of wimp was I? I hated getting things wrong, not that this phobia has ever stopped me messing up and generally failing to be perfect. I laughed recently when a dear friend sent me a card saying, 'I've learnt a lot from my mistakes, so I think I'm going to make some more,' although I can't for the life of me think why she thought I might enjoy it!

Shame

What interests me in the story is the part shame and punishment played in its impact upon me, and whether or not that was all to the good.

'Shame' is an uncomfortable word. None of us like to feel it, but it's one of those emotions that brings us up short and forces us to consider the folly of our ways. Had I and my fellow trespassers not been 'found out' we would have continued taking this exciting route home. What we were doing was not really of great consequence and, renowned as I was for knowing right from wrong, I had not considered it a major misdemeanour until Mr Pledger suggested otherwise. Public exposure brought home to me the fact that my behaviour was found wanting by my community and I was filled with shame.

Shame is not uniformly experienced. My brother did not feel ashamed in the way I did. Despite us being raised in the same household with the same values, he was less bothered by being caught and publicly brought to book for this escapade. Temperamentally he was more laid back and wasn't fussed about having the approval of others. More latterly, when I was a school chaplain I noticed that while some students felt awful about getting detentions, for others they were a badge of honour. Among some there was competition to see who could get the most!

What is considered to be right or wrong varies according to the person you are. Family values and the rules of the society in which you live help to determine what you do or do not find acceptable, as does the stake you feel you have in your community. During the Tottenham riots in August 2011 rioters threw petrol bombs at police, torched vehicles and buildings and looted local shops. In *The Guardian* at the time Lara Oyedele, then CEO of the Odu-Dua housing association, north London, wrote about a generation of young people, like those rioting, who didn't have much hope for their lives:

> The looting doesn't surprise me: it's entertainment, something to keep young people busy. It's not right, but those are the facts. Simply, if they had to go to work this morning they wouldn't have been rioting last night. They're disaffected, unhappy and upset, and they are looking at the likes of me, saying: you need to give me something, I need a job, I need you to help me.
>
> Local communities can only do so much. We can't solve this problem alone. But as long as the situation stays the same, we're going to have more riots on the streets because there are too many angry young people thinking they have no future.[1]

Few of the rioters felt they had anything to lose. They had little conscience about the violence and the looting because they had little sense of belonging to, and being valued by, their community. Herd mentality was activated, with the feeling that since so many of their peers were caught up in the riots it was somehow OK to cause all the damage they did, to wreck the livelihoods of local traders and to take what they wanted.

It's not only those who are disaffected who feel no shame when they breach the laws and standards expected by society. The sexual ethics of the Bloomsbury Group I wrote about in Chapter 14 differed greatly from the publicly accepted norms of their time, but they embraced these values because they found the sexual ethics of wider society to be hypocritical, humanly damaging and irrational. They didn't impose their own way of seeing things on others, just as they would not accept others imposing values they thought unacceptable upon them.

I guess our sense of shame depends upon whether we believe we have fallen short of our own standards, how much we value the opinion of those who are ashamed of us, and whether we believe they are right to be disappointed or condemning of us. Because being shamed can be deeply traumatizing, the fear of it can have an inhibitory impact with consequences that can be positive or negative. If it prevents us doing something harmful to others, that is surely good. If it prevents us standing up to be counted when we're in the minority standing against harmful policies, that's bad news.

Changing values

Over the years I've listened to many people, some of whom feel shame about experiences and personal perspectives that I do not think warrant those feelings, while others have no conscience about actions and attitudes I think are highly questionable. My subjective judgements are not absolutes. I'm no guru able to give definitive answers. I can only listen, try to ask the right questions and, where appropriate, share something of my own journey and what I've learnt to date. Individually and collectively we buy into particular moral values, ethical standpoints and codes of conduct, few of which are unchanging or common to all creeds and cultures in all times. My own moral compass has altered direction at many points in my life as I've learnt more about myself, human experience in general and the complex world we inhabit. It's not that I believe anything goes. I don't, but even where I think something is clearly wrong, the criticism or condemnation that rises in my mind is now usually coupled with compassion arising in my heart because I know most of us don't live in ideal circumstances, life is complicated and decisions aren't always clear-cut.

Throughout this book I've highlighted the gap between our aspirations to live with humanity and our actual reality which involves accepting the capacity in each of us for inhumanity. As a very dear friend once wrote to me in an email when I was struggling with the disparity between the lovely perceptions people have of me and the mess I sometimes am, you ARE inspirational and energising and I also count myself EXTREMELY lucky to have you as my friend – but you're like all of us, strong and capable and wise and kind while at the same time pathetically insecure, needy, selfish, and ruthless. And every other attractive and unattractive aspect of behaviour or emotion you can think of. I think it's called 'being human'...?

Moving on

So where does recognizing and understanding the gap between aspiration and actuality get us? Does it change our focus, our thinking and our behaviour in any useful way? My immediate response to that question is to say it makes life both harder and easier. Easier, because we stop trying to be what we're not – perfect! There's relief in discovering we're not the only person wrestling with questions, impulses and uncertainties we previously thought we were alone in having. We can get on with the task of exploring and understanding these things instead of using up energy pretending we're not the complicated people we are, and building defences of all kinds, emotional and otherwise, to prevent others seeing who we really are. On the other hand, things become harder because seeing life in black and white terms is much simpler than getting to grips with the shades of grey that constantly challenge the certainties we may rely on for our sense of security. Wrestling with complexity takes effort, energy, courage, time, rigorous self-honesty and a capacity to question, gently and incisively, the black and white thinking that can so often be a source of oppression.

Consequences

My own perspective has subtly shifted away from focusing on the 'rights' and 'wrongs' of any given situation. I want to know instead how human well-being will be or has been affected by the choices made and, when people are harmed (psychologically or physically) by such choices, how the well-being of those involved will be affected by our response to the damage caused. It's about trying to make wise judgements rather than being judgemental; thinking more in terms of consequences rather than knee-jerk condemnation.

Two questions become critical here. They have been present implicitly and explicitly in every chapter of this book. What of our human experience rightly should remain private and what should become part of the public domain? When is retributive justice appropriate and when is restorative justice a better way forward when we harm others and ourselves, as we all do, to varying degrees and at different times in our life?

Privacy vs public scrutiny

I shall deal first with the private/public balance. This naturally leads into reflections about forms of justice. What should be kept private and what should be made public is a question we have to grapple with in many areas of human experience, and not simply in relation to human failure and fallibility. An example from the field of scientific research illustrates well some of the issues.

In February 2013 the White House moved to increase public access to taxpayer-funded scientific research. They were responding to a 'We the People' e-petition demanding free online access to taxpayer-funded research. The benefits of public accessibility are clear. In December 2012 15-year-old Jack Andraka announced he had invented a diagnostic test for pancreatic cancer. It cost three cents to have done and is a significantly faster and more accurate test than the best tests already available. Without online open access to relevant research papers Jack would not have been able to read such material, even if he had been able to locate it. He would not have been able to afford the subscriptions giving him access to articles in the necessary scientific journals.

In June 2012 the Wellcome Trust, the second largest research charity in the world, announced it would withhold funding from scientists who were not prepared to make the results of their research freely available to the public, although this didn't seem to apply to privately funded research.

While the positive aspects of making scientific research accessible and preventing pharmaceutical companies, for example, from claiming patents that prevent people accessing the medicines they need, either because of lack of availability or financial constraint, are clear, the matter is not clear-cut. If research is privately funded, and the investors require a return on their investment, however much they want to help make advances in research that saves lives, is it appropriate that they should bear the costs but not reap any financial reward because the results of their investment are made publicly accessible? Philanthropists who make donations without expecting or needing any financial reward are exceptions rather than the rule. Is there a balance to be struck between the greater public good and enabling investors to profit from their investments? If there is no return, will investment cease and the speed of research slow down?

Secrecy and national security

The matter becomes more complicated when we consider issues of national security. What if publicly funded scientific research in the field of national security were to jeopardize national security if it was made public? Who determines jeopardy and whether a particular area of research is both necessary and ethically acceptable as a means of maintaining national security? The diversity of reactions to the leaks of Julian Assange and, later, Edward Snowden suggests that public opinion is divided about whether those taking such decisions in secret are getting things right. Who should know if government agencies are using technology to breach internationally agreed 'rules of engagement' for the purposes of 'preserving national security', and how?

When Edward Snowden leaked details of several top-secret US and British government mass-surveillance programmes to the press he defended his actions by claiming they were intended 'to inform the public as to that which is done in their name and that which is done against them'.[2] For some he was a whistle-blower exposing wrongdoing. For others he was a dissident, a traitor or a patriot.

Snowden's leaks had major international implications but, unlike many global news stories, his revelations also unsettled our personal sense of security. As with the *News of the World* phone-hacking scandal for which Metropolitan Police investigations began as far back as 1999, we were discovering that what we had previously understood to be private means of communication were open to the actions of hackers. The private sphere suddenly seemed to be shrinking rapidly, prompting sometimes hypocritical as well as concerned reactions. While many were happy to read about the 'private' lives of those in the public eye, they were not happy about the potential for others secretly to invade their own privacy.

Questions

1 What are your experiences of being shamed or shaming others?
2 What difference does it make to think in terms of consequences instead of right and wrong?
3 Would you want your faults and failings to be as publicly exposed as you want the faults and failings of others to be?

18

Retributive and restorative justice

What in our own private lives needs to be made public? Our response to this question has altered significantly over the last century. 'Airing your dirty laundry in public' was once regarded as un-British and vulgar. The stiff upper lip was a sign of fortitude, courage, even virtue. Today, while this attitude persists in places, we have undergone a cultural revolution that first took a swipe at the stiff upper lip and drew blood during the 1960s when all kinds of previously unquestioned attitudes bit the dust. The pill triggered a sexual revolution. Post-war teenagers no longer conformed to family patterns. Colourful, informal, sexually provocative fashions and increasingly loud and rebellious music reflected a sea-change in attitudes about what was and what was not acceptable. Greater prosperity and access to international travel, the arrival of new and diverse cultures into British society, and technological and scientific advancement opened up the world almost more quickly than we could psychologically adjust to the changes.

Letting it all hang out

Within the last decade, far from airing your dirty laundry in public being seen as something to be avoided, it has become the norm for many, particularly among those born as one millennium ended and another began. Given half a chance, school students will happily text the trivial details of their day, as well as every development of their latest teenage drama as it unfolds. Reality TV has encouraged people not to hold back on holding forth and revealing their innermost secrets. Facebook and other social media sites have become modern-day confessionals and gossip columns connecting users not only with family and friends but also strangers who may not be all they say they are.

Some people began to have second thoughts about being so publicly accessible when they did not get jobs because their prospective employer had taken the trouble to look up their Facebook page and had not been impressed by what they saw, or they lost their job because of indiscreet comments they had made on publicly accessible online social media sites. Alarm bells began to ring when online bullying led to depression and, tragically, suicide among teenagers, or evidence appeared of paedophiles using these sites to groom vulnerable youngsters. Celebrities and other public figures happily tweeting away learnt through painful experience that the ability to communicate with their public via such means was a double-edged sword, enabling those who adored them to contact them obsessively, and their detractors and other mad, lonely, inadequate individuals to slander and threaten them with seeming impunity. Maybe letting it all hang out was not such a great idea after all.

Selective sharing

Discussing our difficulties with other people may well be helpful, particularly when we discover in doing so that we are not alone in the struggles we have, but in sharing confidences we need to be confident that our openness will not be abused and to do so in safe and appropriate spaces. Years ago the Jesuit John Powell wrote a wonderful, and now out of print book asking the question, *Why am I afraid to tell you who I am?* Put simply, the answer went along the lines of, 'I am afraid to tell you who I am because you may not like who I am and it's all I've got.' We are right to be careful in our choice of those with whom we share our deepest and most damaged selves. It can be a cruel world and revealing who we are to the wrong people can leave us more damaged and demoralized than ever.

We may now have the world at our computer fingertips and be able to communicate in a month with more people than our great-grandparents did in a lifetime, but the 'places' where we feel able to be truly ourselves seem to be disappearing. 'Lonely' is how increasing numbers of people who come to see me describe their lives. They may be the life and soul of the party as far as their friends are concerned, or they may find relating to others difficult. They may live in a remote place, or be surrounded by anonymous crowds in the city. But loneliness is common to them all. I know that state myself. It's not about being with people, but about understanding and being understood by people. I suspect many of us will identify with these lyrics from a song by Ken Medema directed at the Church:

> If this is not a place, where tears are understood
> Where can I go to cry?
> And if this is not a place, where spirit can take wing
> Where can I go to fly?

I don't need another place, for trying to impress you,
With just how good and virtuous I am
I don't need another place, for always being on top of things
Ev'rybody knows that it's a sham
I don't need another place, for always wearing smiles
Even when it's not the way I feel
I don't need another place, to mouth the same old platitudes
'Cause you and I both know, that it's not real

If this is not a place, where my questions can be asked
Where shall I go to seek?
And if this is not a place, where my heart cries can be heard
Where shall I go to speak?

I don't need another place, for trying to impress you,
With just how good and virtuous I am
I don't need another place, for always being on top of things
Ev'rybody knows that it's a sham
I don't need another place, for always wearing smiles
Even when it's not the way I feel
I don't need another place, to mouth the same old platitudes
'Cause you and I both know, that it's not real

If this is not a place, where tears are understood
Where shall I go, where shall I go to fly?[1]

At a personal level we need to find those people and, possibly, communities that provide the 'place' Ken Medema seeks. When we choose to make public what is private, albeit to one person, we need to know that the person in whom we are placing our confidence will help, not harm us further.

Finding the balance

At the beginning of the book I said that when I had been the cause of hurt to someone else what I most needed was a safe space in which to deal with the harm I'd caused and the personal issues thrown up by what I had said or done. My sense is that in every situation where harm has been done we will need to hold the tension between there being enough public exposure, if that is necessary, to make the one causing harm see and take responsibility for what they've done, while enabling the privacy necessary for those harmed, and the one who has done the harm, to recover their lives and learn from the mistakes made.

Thinking back to the simple example I gave of my brother and me and the hospital 'assault course', it was necessary for hospital staff and patients to complain, and for Mr Pledger to say what we'd done was wrong, in order for me to realize I'd been doing something that was not considered appropriate. I do not think the boys needed to stand humiliated for all to see in the school playground or assembly hall in order to understand their error and choose not to do it again.

Proportionate responses

My sense is that in any situation where what Professor Mervyn Frost calls 'ethical fouls' have been committed, the people who need to know are those who have been harmed or who may be harmed if they are not informed. Public exposure in the national and international media about the phone-hacking scandal, the financial crisis, failures of care in the NHS and care homes, and the MPs' misuse of expenses, was reasonable to expect because the general public were impacted upon, or could be affected, by what had happened in those situations. They raised questions about personal and collective responsibility and about what is or is not reasonable to expect of those we ask to act in our name, and what values we want to guide how we work together.

On the other hand, unless publicity will help to solve a particular crime or lead to changes in law or practice that will prevent tragedies, I am not sure it is necessary for the general public to know about them. Imagine if you are the close relative of a person who has died in an accident or been murdered. The grief of that is more than enough to cope with. To have photographers and journalists camped on your doorstep, wanting to interview you every time you step out of the house would be profoundly traumatic, not only making it harder for those bereaved to deal with their grief, but also harming them further. Why do we accept others being harassed in this way, simply for the sake of a 'good story', when we would hate for it to happen to us, and in some cases it serves little or no purpose in bringing deeper understanding?

When well-known people foul up in their personal lives, to what extent should they be publicly exposed? I think those who are harmed by their actions have a right to know and understand the situation, but why should anyone else have access to the information? Privacy is needed so that the problems can be dealt with by those concerned in the best way possible. Put in the same situation, what would we and our families need?

Justice

At the beginning of this book I said that when I had been harmed by the actions of another person one of the things I needed was for them to 'pay a price' for what they'd done. I was once in a situation where a senior colleague behaved unprofessionally in a way that caused me a great deal of distress. He knew, as did others who were involved, that he had got things wrong, but I chose not to make a formal complaint. I wanted to use my energy more positively, and I was conscious of my own fallibility, so I wanted to find a way of responding that took account of these things. For a couple of months the person concerned carried on in his position as if nothing had happened, and the injustice of this stole my peace of mind, preventing me from laying the situation to rest and moving on.

With this in mind I can understand why, when terrible acts like murder have been committed, those bereaved cannot get on with their lives until the murderer is caught and receives a sentence that takes seriously the harm done. I am conscious of how punishment of the perpetrator – retributive justice – may not only be needed by those harmed but may also be of benefit to the guilty party. Contrary to popular opinion, not everyone who ends up in prison is confirmed further in their criminal frame of mind. For some it is a positive turning point which, if and when they are released, enables them to live a different way of life than the one that brought them into prison. To have one's life taken, whether through being illegally murdered on the street or by legal, lethal injection in a state penitentiary (is the latter not equally murder?), is unacceptable. In both cases the opportunity to grow, change and develop is curtailed. Supporting the death penalty as a means of punishment for homicide removes any possibility of redeeming the evil done in any way, and I'm not always sure it provides the justice that is critically needed.

The bigger picture

In December 2012 a 23-year-old woman and her boyfriend were attacked on a bus in Delhi and the woman violently gang-raped by five men, four adults and a juvenile. When the judge sentenced the four adults to death, women keeping vigil outside the court danced in the street. I understood their elation but I could not dance. Somehow it seemed to me these men were being scapegoated for the 'sins' of a cultural, religious and social context that had taught and accepted for centuries the second-class position of women and turned a blind eye to sexual harassment and assault. *Invisible Women*, a report by academics Shilpa Phadke, Shilpa Ranade and Sameera Khan, which came out shortly after the men were sentenced, expressed a real concern that with the ending of the Delhi trial, media attention would move elsewhere and the mistreatment of women and its deep-seated causes would continue as before.

Justice will not have been done in changing misogynistic beliefs and India's infrastructure to create a safer society for women simply through hanging four men who were caught, tried and found guilty of this particularly awful gang-rape. At the very least there is a need for restorative justice alongside retributive responses.

Restorative vs retributive justice

Restorative justice is what I want and need when I have wronged another. Retributive justice doesn't necessarily bring restoration. It can make the latter harder for a time, even impossible. At a human level restoration is essential for well-being, and history teaches us that where psychological wounds remain unhealed in victims and perpetrators alike, peace will always be under threat from further inhumanity. Knowing my own differing needs in relation to restorative and retributive justice, according to whether I am the one harmed or the one guilty of harming, I must take seriously what each of these demands in terms of privacy or publicity. In relation to the colleague whose unprofessional actions caused me distress I could acknowledge my desire for him to be publicly exposed and deposed, but in terms of the action I chose I wanted to be mindful of what I would need to help me make amends when I get things wrong.

Giving time, time

There's a story concerning the sons of Isaac, one of the patriarchs of the Hebrew Scriptures. Isaac is old, frail and blind and the time has come for him to pass on his blessing to his elder son, Esau. Esau is one of twins, born minutes before his brother Jacob. Years later, Rebekah helps her favourite son, Jacob, deceive Isaac into giving Jacob the blessing that is rightfully Esau's. In effect this places Esau into the service of his brother, a situation that cannot be undone. The family is torn apart. Isaac is grieved by the deception of his wife and younger son. Esau plots to kill Jacob. Rebekah has to send away Jacob to live with her brother Laban.

Jacob is exiled for many years, during which time he is on the receiving end of a similar deception to that which he imposed on his father. Laban tricks him into marrying Leah when his love is for her sister Rachel. He must serve Laban for a further seven years in order to have Rachel as his wife as well. Eventually Jacob and Laban find sharing the same space impossible. Jacob flees with all his family, flocks and possessions, resolving to return home. Laban follows in hot pursuit. Violent conflict seems imminent but the two men manage some honest dialogue and come to a mutual agreement. Jacob is allowed to continue on his way. He is fearful of confronting Esau after all these years. He wrestles all night by the Ford of Jabbok with a character who puts his hip out of joint and who Jacob comes to see as 'the face of God'.

The essential need for privacy

The journey home represents a psychological journey away from patterns of rivalry, deception, family breakdown and violence to purposeful self-examination, transformation and, ultimately, restoration with his twin, Esau. So many of the dynamics of the story reflect our own human failings, conflicts and capacities to learn from hard experience and finally to come home to ourselves, restoring that which has been broken in the process. This change cannot be rushed. Friends and colleagues who once served many years in prison for murder but now do amazing work with the victims and perpetrators of violent conflict did not make that transformation overnight, nor have they reached the end point of their personal journey. Their need for solitary space to work with the legacy of their violence remains crucial. Change would never have been possible under the constant and continuous spotlight of condemnatory public attention.

Time and again when I meet with men and women who have committed violent acts, and I learn their stories, I think about how I might have grown up if I had walked in their shoes experiencing their pain. I think too about how, despite all the privileges of life and love I have been lucky enough to have, I have hurt others along the way, sometimes badly. You may recognize that reality in your own experience. We all need safe private spaces in which to lick our wounds, regroup, remember what has happened in order to be re-membered (that is, put back together again), learn from our mistakes and continue along the way with other wounded healers who are also a mix of beauty and brokenness.

Now what?

Whenever Chris, I or our children say the words 'Now what?', the others all respond with a panicked 'Aaaaaah!' I can't remember where that weird family tradition began, but as I approach the end of this book and pose the same question, 'Aaaaaah!' seems an understandable response. After all, while mapping out a little of the landscape of human messiness, I've offered few, if any, answers to the questions this quagmire of experience throws up.

I've given no get-out clauses to avoid the pitfalls of being imperfect, nor suggested any short cuts to finding the positive power of imperfection while avoiding the pain of it. I've undermined the legitimacy of black and white thinking and the comforting certainty that comes with it. I've stated that while we prefer to consider the problems we face and the responsibility to deal with them as belonging to someone else, we aren't guilt-free and the buck stops as much with us to sort them out as with those we consider more culpable. All in all it looks like this book won't have a neat and happy ending because to all intents and purposes it seems we are now stuck up the creek of human complexity without a paddle . . . Aaaaaah!

On the other hand, if we stop fighting against the current of our imperfections and go with the flow, learning to ride the wave of human reality instead of being pulled down and overwhelmed by it, life might well be less exhausting and become more exhilarating, particularly when we discover we're not alone in the adventure. The burden of trying to be what we're not, of feeling that everyone has things more sussed than we do, is lifted. Free to look up, we see not only all those destructive, damaging, diminishing and demented aspects of our inhumanity, but also their potential to be the positive energy that takes us forward. Or, to use an image for those of you who prefer to keep your feet on dry land, our messy human experience becomes the dirt-compost in which the seeds of creativity, vibrant 'colour' and compassion can take root, germinate, grow and flourish. The way forward doesn't lie in pretending to be what we are not, but in working compassionately with who we are. We can see ourselves as a 'work in progress', with each day bringing new opportunities for creative transformation. This may be the end of the book but it's far from being the end of the story. Nothing may have changed except our perception of reality, but that changes everything.

Questions

1 What do you need when you have been hurt and when you have hurt another person?
2 Do your attitudes about what is just differ when it's you seeking justice or someone seeking justice from you?
3 How can you help society create the kind of safe spaces where we can be honest and work together for greater healing?

Notes

1 Paradise lost

1 Brian McCabe, *One Atom to Another*, Edinburgh: Polygon, 1987.
2 Richard Rohr, *Falling Upward*, London: SPCK, 2012, p. xx.
3 Michael Ondaatje, *The English Patient*, London: Picador, 1992, p. 261.
4 Kahlil Gibran, *The Prophet*, London: William Heinemann, 1980, p. 61.

2 Life after Eden

1 Tennessee Williams, *Conversations with Tennessee Williams*, ed. Albert J. Devlin, Jackson, MS: University Press of Mississippi, 1986.
2 Monica Furlong, *God's a Good Man and Other Poems*, Oxford: A. R. Mowbray and Co., 1974, p. 62.
3 Rachel Joyce, *The Unlikely Pilgrimage of Harold Fry*, London: Doubleday, 2012, p. 106.
4 <www.sayakaganz.com>.

3 Tools for the journey

1 Iain McGilchrist, *The Master and His Emissary*, New Haven, CT: Yale University Press, 2009.
2 James Hollis, *Finding Meaning in the Second Half of Life*, New York: Gotham Books, 2006.
3 Rowan Williams, *Faith in the Public Square*, London: Bloomsbury, 2012, p. 213.

4 No man is an island

1 <http://www.tutufoundationuk.org/ubuntu.php>.

5 Community challenge

1 Richard Holloway, *Leaving Alexandria*, Edinburgh: Canongate, 2012, p. 220.

7 What's yours is mine!

1 Richard Rohr, *Falling Upward*, London: SPCK, 2012, p. 69.

8 Our blinded sight

1 Susan Cain, *Quiet*, London: Penguin, 2012, p. 84.
2 'Neurological Correlates of Social Conformity and Independence During Mental Rotation', *Journal of Biological Psychiatry* 2005:58, pp. 245–53.
3 Hannah Arendt, *Eichmann in Jerusalem: A Report on the Banality of Evil*, London: Penguin, 1977.

4 Rowan Williams, *Faith in the Public Square*, London: Bloomsbury, 2012, p. 224.

10 The cost of caring

1 Naomi Shihab Nye, *Words Under the Words: Selected Poems*, Portland, OR: The Eighth Mountain Press, 1994.

11 No peace in our time

1 Morgan Scott Peck, *The Road Less Travelled*, New York: Simon & Schuster, 1978.
2 Rowan Williams, *Faith in the Public Square*, London: Bloomsbury, 2012.

12 Faith in conflict

1 Viktor Frankl, *Man's Search for Meaning*, New York: Washington Square Press, 1959, p. 86.
2 Alistair Little and Ruth Scott, *Give a Boy a Gun*, London: Darton, Longman & Todd, 2009.
3 Eric Symes Abbott, *Invitations to Prayer: Selections from the Writings of Eric Symes Abbott, Dean of Westminster, 1959–1974*, Cincinnati, OH: Forward Movement Publications, 1989, p. 83.

14 Where is love?

1 John Cornwell, *The Dark Box*, Profile Books, 2014, p. 20.
2 Cornwell, *The Dark Box*, p. 21.
3 John Gray, *Men are from Mars, Women are from Venus*, London: Harper Element, 1992.
4 <http://interfaithenabler.blogspot.co.uk/2012/06/jesus-divorce-and-equal-marriage-rabbi.html>.
5 <http://www.psychologytoday.com/articles/200505/marriage-history>.
6 Frances Partridge, *Memories*, London: Phoenix, 1981, p. 154.
7 Partridge, *Memories*, p. 76.
8 Partridge, *Memories*, pp. 117–18.
9 David Whyte, *Fire in the Earth*, Langley, WA: Many Rivers Press, 1992.

15 How are the mighty fallen

1 Kenneth Steven, *Iona: Poems*, Edinburgh: St Andrew Press, 2000, p. 16.
2 Sara Maitland, *A Book of Silence*, London: Granta, 2008, p. 117.
3 Maitland, *A Book of Silence*, p. 117.
4 Iain McGilchrist, *The Master and His Emissary*, New Haven, CT: Yale University Press, 2009, p. 105.
5 McGilchrist, *The Master and His Emissary*, p. 106.
6 McGilchrist, *The Master and His Emissary*, p. 113.
7 Helen Luke, *Old Age: Journey into Simplicity*, New York: Parabola Books, 1987, p. 4.
8 Luke, *Old Age*, p. 5.

16 True power

1 *The Guardian*, 19 August 2013.
2 *The Guardian*, 20 August 2013.
3 John Ralston Saul, *Voltaire's Bastards: The Dictatorship of Reason in the West*, New York: Vintage Books, 1992.
4 Jacques Maritain, *Man and the State*, University of Chicago Press, 1951, pp. 108ff.

17 Justice or just us?

1 <theguardian.com>, 9 August 2011.
2 *The Guardian*, 'Edward Snowden: the whistleblower behind the NSA surveillance revelations', 9 June 2013.

18 Retributive and restorative justice

1 <http://kenmedema.com/ifthisisnotaplacedownload.aspx>.

Copyright acknowledgements

Did you know that SPCK is a registered charity?

As well as publishing great books by leading Christian authors, we also . . .

. . . make assemblies meaningful and fun for over a million children by running www.assemblies.org.uk, a popular website that provides free assembly scripts for teachers. For many children, school assembly is the only contact they have with Christian faith and culture, and the only time in their week for spiritual reflection.

. . . help prisoners become confident readers with our easy-to-read stories. Poor literacy is a huge barrier to rehabilitation. Prisoners identify with the believable heroes of our gritty fiction, but questions at the end of each chapter help them to examine their choices from a moral perspective and to build their reading confidence.

. . . support student ministers overseas in their training. We give them free, specially written theology books, the International Study Guides. These books really do make a difference, not just to students but to ministers and, through them, to a whole community.

Please support these great schemes: visit www.spck.org.uk/support-us to find out more.